Current Approaches
Breaking Bad News

Edited by
J Couriel, R Hull and
V J Harten-Ash

**duphar
medical relations**

First published 1989

ISBN 1–870678–16–8

Produced by PSA Print Services

CONTENTS

FOREWORD

The ability to communicate clearly and sensitively is an essential aspect of good clinical practice. Nowhere are the skills of listening and speaking needed more than when imparting the diagnosis of a fatal illness or handicap to patients and their relatives. It is clear that the manner in which this news is broken has a profound influence on the way they will subsequently react to the diagnosis.

Although the importance of learning such communication skills is widely recognised, many students and doctors receive little or no teaching on this subject during their training. That the subject is of interest to a wide range of disciplines, was demonstrated by the size and vitality of the audience that attended a Symposium entitled 'Breaking Bad News', held at the Royal College of Physicians in London, in January 1989. The audience included physicians, paediatricians, general practitioners, psychologists, students and allied professionals. This book is a summary of that meeting.

The first presentations dealt with three difficult and common problems in paediatrics: breaking the news of a congenital abnormality, or of an unexpected death, to parents, and talking to children about their life-threatening illness. There followed two views, from a psychologist and from a physician, of the special needs of patients diagnosed as being HIV-positive. The ways in which we can teach and learn about more effective communication were explored in the afternoon session.

By the end of the meeting, several important and common themes had emerged. The first was that patients and their relatives need, want, and deserve to be told the truth about their illnesses. Patronising euphemisms are no longer acceptable. The second was that if doctors are to be able to talk more honestly and sensitively, they will need a better understanding of what the diagnosis means to an individual patient, than many possess. Techniques such as role play, simulated patients, video recordings and small group discussions offer exciting alternatives to the traditional bedside apprenticeship. But perhaps the clearest message from this stimulating Symposium was that we can all improve our ability to listen to the needs of those we care for.

JON COURIEL
Consultant Paediatrician
Booth Hall Children's Hospital
Manchester

INTRODUCING PARENTS TO THEIR ABNORMAL BABY

Dr Richard G Pearse MA MB BChir FRCP
Consultant Neonatal Paediatrician
The Jessop Hospital for Women, Sheffield

One in 40 babies is born with a major abnormality and yet we really know very little about how to tell the parents about this. That we need to learn how to do so and that we are not effective at doing it, is clear from Hogg's study in which he showed that 80% of the parents of severely retarded children did not remember ever having been told officially about the retardation.[1]

Childbirth is a very emotional occasion for parents. If the baby is abnormal, additional very complex emotions arise and the process of the birth may be regarded as useless. The labour and delivery are almost always considered by the parents to have been difficult if the end result of the labour is a dead or deformed baby. The whole situation is made more difficult for the parents by the attitudes and reactions of the people around them. The professionals, whether they be doctors, nurses or midwives, may be less ready to go and talk to the mother of an abnormal baby than to the mother of a normal baby. The parents of an abnormal baby are very sensitive and will notice this and interpret it as being shunned. A pregnant mother gets generalised public approval with comments such as 'You look radiant' or 'Pregnancy suits you', with people going out of their way to talk to them and ask them how they are. However, if the baby is deformed or dies, word gets around the community, and people do not know what to say to the mother and so avoid her. They may also be wondering what the mother did wrong to cause the deformity or to deserve it happening to her.

There are basically three situations in which bad news has to be brought to parents.

The first, which is becoming more common, is where an abnormality has been detected on antenatal ultrasound scan. This group of patients can be divided into three subgroups where:

(i) The diagnosis is clear and the advice is to terminate the pregnancy (e.g. anencephaly)
(ii) The diagnosis is clear but the pregnancy should be allowed to continue without intervention (e.g. a cardiac or gut anomaly) or much more rarely with intervention, e.g. 'intrauterine surgery' (e.g. posterior urethral valves)

or

(iii) The diagnosis is unclear, but there is a definite abnormality of unknown significance.

There are particular problems about telling parents about abnormalities on ultrasound scans. It is often difficult for the professionals to be sure of what they are seeing. This uncertainty is bound to be, and should be, conveyed to the parents. We have only our own collection of slides and textbook pictures to help us in our description and we are not all able to draw a good representation of what we think we see. It is not clear whether one should start with a picture of a small lesion and say 'your baby's problem is like this, but bigger' or start with a picture of a huge lesion and say 'your baby's problem is like this but a lot smaller'.

Finding an abnormality on antenatal ultrasound scan will inevitably cause considerable anxiety in the parents. However, with patient, unhurried explanation, this anxiety can be alleviated to some extent. The knowledge gained from the scan does, however, have the great advantage of allowing the delivery to be planned so that the timing, place and mode of delivery can be chosen. This will optimise the chances for the baby. It also allows us to discuss with the parents whether or not to do an emergency Caesarean section if there is fetal distress, and whether or not to resuscitate the baby. This avoids inexperienced junior medical staff having to make instant decisions about these matters in the middle of the night.

The second situation where parents need to be told bad news is where a previously undiagnosed abnormality becomes evident at birth. Such an abnormality may or may not be evident to the parents. If the abnormality is obvious, then the professional attending the delivery will have to give a simple explanation of the abnormality. If it is not obvious to the parents, then I think that they should be told as soon as possible by the most senior person available. If the professionals attending the delivery are unsure of the diagnosis, e.g. in a baby with suspected Down's Syndrome, then the Consultant Paediatrician should be called to confirm or refute the diagnosis.

The third sort of situation which arises is where the abnormality becomes obvious to the professional in the course of the first days or weeks, e.g. after perinatal asphyxia when normal feeding does not become established. It is very difficult for these parents to believe that what their child is doing is not just a variant of normal and temporary behaviour, as to them the baby looks and acts normally. They may try to find plausible excuses for why their baby is behaving as it is. They may also put an inordinate amount of weight on the child achieving one of the milestones which have been mentioned as pointers to an underlying chronic problem. For instance, the fact that an asphyxiated baby finally successfully bottle feeds may be interpreted by the parents that the baby has become normal and that the damage has been repaired or that the diagnosis was always wrong.

2

THE METHOD OF TELLING

1. Where to say it

If possible the parents should be told together. It must be in a quiet room where there will be no interruptions. One other professional can be present, preferably one who has already been involved with the parents. If more are present then this can inhibit the parents from voicing their most intimate fears. If the mother is single and the boyfriend is no longer important to her, then somebody else who matters to her, such as her mother or a close friend, should be encouraged to be present.

If the baby has already been delivered, then it is best to tell them with the baby in their arms. If the baby is still in utero then ideally they should be shown the scan or a recording or picture of the scan during the interview.

2. What to say

Parents are usually aware that there are problems because they are very sensitive to the atmosphere and will see from the faces of the professionals that the news is bad. It is unnecessarily cruel to walk into the room with them and to then start beating about the bush. It is important to tell the truth. After introducing yourself, you should begin with a brief and simple explanation of the problems, pointing out those features which make you think that their baby is abnormal. A balanced view of the significance of your diagnosis for the baby and themselves should be presented. This should be neither over-optimistic nor over-pessimistic. They should be given something positive to hang onto, so that they can have some hopes even in the most hopeless and awful situation and also have something to be proud of. There is a phase through which we almost all pass, when inexperienced, in which we paint a picture as black as possible when explaining problems to parents, to make sure that we have got the message across. This is unnecessary because parents can become too depressed and they have enough to cope with. A balanced explanation, without getting too involved in all the details of the special needs that the baby may have in the future, is all that is required at first. For the first six months the parents will probably only need to give their child what any other baby would need—love, food, warmth and a clean nappy. Later the parents will find out what the particular needs of their child are and will have to adjust to these as they become aware of them.

It is also important, even in the first interview, to try to allay the feelings of guilt that the parents, particularly the mother, may have. Parents almost always feel that they have done something wrong, either during the pregnancy to cause the problems or in their 'murky pasts', for which this is punishment.

They may also feel very guilty about their reaction to the abnormality

3

and their feelings of rejection and possibly revulsion. These feelings should be talked about openly. They will be discussed in more detail later.

3. How to say it

It is important that the parents are given frequent short interviews rather than that they are 'told all' in one long interview. They usually only take in one or two facts and then do not hear anything else for the rest of that interview. Having told the parents in the initial interview, you should give them time alone for the information to sink in and return over the first few hours to answer any questions and to go over any important points again.

You should talk to them looking them straight in the eye. Parents rightly complain if they are told the bad news while the doctor is looking out of the window or fiddling with his pen. They need to be told sympathetically and humanely. If you want to put your arm round them, they are not going to charge you with assault. If you want to cry with them, they will not object or think any the less of you.

It is also helpful if you see both parents individually at a later stage. The father particularly may have special fears about his wife which he cannot express in front of her. They may both have fears about the baby which they do not want to mention in front of their partner because they do not want to worry them further. There may also be things about which they feel very guilty, but which they have withheld from the partner, such as a previous termination of pregnancy or an episode of venereal disease in the past, which they may feel has caused the problem in some way.

4. When to say it

In the past, many professionals have advocated waiting before telling the bad news. I have even heard of one paediatrician who waited nine months before imparting the diagnosis of Down's Syndrome to some parents. This attitude probably stems from two main concerns. Firstly, there is a feeling that it may be a good idea to allow parents to bond with their baby and to give them a period of blissful ignorance when they can enjoy their baby before facing up to reality. Secondly, I think that the motive may be just putting off the very unpleasant task of telling the parents—and it is never pleasant—in the hope that it will not be necessary: unnecessary either because the parents have noticed the problem for themselves or because another professional has told them.

In a study of parents who had been told the diagnosis of Down's Syndrome in their baby at least one week after the diagnosis had been made, Cunningham showed that this delay was a major cause of

4

complaint.[2] Parents found it acceptable to delay giving the diagnosis only if the mother was extremely ill after delivery, if the diagnosis was genuinely uncertain and chromosome results were awaited, or if it was impossible to see the parents together.

Personally, I do not usually wait for chromosome results, but express my suspicions to the parents on clinical grounds alone, if I am reasonably certain of the diagnosis. I will go into the hospital even in the early hours of the morning to tell parents that their baby has Down's Syndrome or whatever the diagnosis is. It seems to be unnecessarily cruel to allow the father to ring round the family with the joyous news that they have a lovely son or daughter and then to have to repeat the call some hours later to say that the baby has Down's Syndrome.

Once they have been told the news parents may want to telephone their families or friends. We have a special quiet sitting room with a telephone in it from which the father or mother can telephone their parents, relatives and friends. They may well want to cry and it is obviously unsympathetic to expect them to use a public call-box in a hospital corridor or even a phone in a busy office or nursing station. Some parents prefer a professional from the hospital to contact the family and so I offer this.

I have been unable to find any research on how the parents of an abnormal baby bring the news to their families. There must be good and bad ways of doing it, but I find it difficult to give them advice on how best to do this. I assume that the same general rules apply as for a professional telling the baby's parents.

SEEING THE BABY

It is extremely important that the parents see their abnormal baby. The human imagination knows almost no bounds and can dream up far more horrific and upsetting abnormalities than anything that nature creates. Once the parents have seen their baby they have a clearer picture in their own mind and this reduces nightmarish flights of fancy.

There are many ways of introducing the parents to their baby. I think that the best way is to do it absolutely naturally, handing the baby to them directly after the delivery as though there was nothing wrong, but as you do so, explaining what the obvious abnormality is. If the professionals involved do not show revulsion and rejection then the parents are less likely to do so.

If the abnormality is considered too shocking then it is best if the baby is wrapped in such a way as to minimise the defect and a brief, simple explanation of the problem given as the baby is handed to them. They should then be given a few minutes alone with their baby in their arms. They will usually unwrap the baby to discover the abnormalities at a speed with which they can cope.

Parents refuse to see their baby most commonly where an abnormality has been noted on an antenatal scan and they have not been properly counselled at the time. If the parents refuse to see their baby, they should be very strongly persuaded to do so for the reasons mentioned above. I have had to bully parents on many occasions to do so and all of those have subsequently thanked me. In my experience neither anencephaly nor even the collapsed skull of a hydrocephalic child delivered by destructive delivery are too horrific if the baby is properly wrapped and the professional's approach is sympathetic. Even severe degrees of maceration do not seem to matter if the parents receive an explanation of what it is. They only seem to see the facial features of their baby.

Should the parents refuse absolutely to see their baby then their wishes should be complied with at the time. They usually do this because they are very frightened. There are a number of ways to help persuade them to see and cuddle their baby and to conquer their fear: by repeated short visits stressing the more positive things about the baby, and by making him or her a person, e.g. 'she's got a lovely face' or 'he's a real fighter' or whatever seems appropriate. If the parents have given the baby a name then this should be used as much as possible in conversation. They should always be strongly persuaded to name their baby so that they can talk about him or her more easily. They should use a favourite name and not keep the name which they were going to use for the next, hopefully normal, baby.

Polaroid pictures should be taken of the baby. If the abnormality is very obvious and upsetting then they should be taken either from very close, so that they are blurred, or from far enough away to make the abnormality less obvious. They should be taken of the baby as a baby and not as one would for a medical textbook. Very often parents can be persuaded to look at pictures of their baby and once they have seen the problem is not as horrific as they imagined, then they will see and cuddle their baby. Parents who refuse even this should be told that pictures of their baby are available, and these should be stored in the notes.

Sometimes one parent can be persuaded to see the baby and can persuade the other to do so in due course. Another technique which occasionally works is to draw the abnormality for the parents. This may just be sufficiently detached for them to be able to cope with and then once they have seen that it is not as bad as their worst fears then they will eventually see their own baby. They may be persuaded to look at pictures of someone else's baby with a similar condition.

Unfortunately there are no books available of pictures of babies who happen to have major defects as babies. The illustrations in medical texts are taken to accentuate the defect and to minimise the baby.

Most parents benefit from receiving some written information about their child's condition. We should try to have something available for the more common conditions. This is no substitute for talking to the parents, but it is useful for them to have something to look at when they feel less shocked and in a more receptive state. They may also use it as a way of opening a discussion with their friends or relatives. Some parents may search the public library or any other soure they can find for information about their child's condition. Unfortunately this information, if and when they find it, is often out of date, and may be totally inappropriate and misleading. It is easy to overload parents with facts because they are articulate, ask penetrating questions and want to know all aspects of their child's condition.

Many parents will benefit from being introduced to other parents of babies with a similar condition. This does not have to be immediately after the birth, but should be offered, if possible, and may be taken up at a later date. There are potential problems because it is very difficult to find two babies who are alike in all aspects of the condition and one may develop a complication that the other does not and this will lead to extra anxiety, e.g. leukaemia in Down's Syndrome.

THE PARENTS' RESPONSES

How do parents react to the news? Cunningham divides their responses into feelings and reactions.[3] 'Feelings' are emotions that endure, they are there all the time and never go away. 'Reactions' are more temporary and are a coping mechanism. There are innumerable feelings, such as guilt, embarrassment, blame, shame, anger, grief, loss, sadness, yearning, futility and many others. Reactions are fewer in number but equally important. Shock is universal. It must be truly shocking to learn that the lovely baby you had been expecting is in fact abnormal. Shock is often rapidly replaced by numbness. This is much like the grief reaction where the parents have blown their emotional fuse and do not feel either happy or sad any more—they just do not feel anything. This may be followed by denial. They deny that this is happening to them. They feel that it must be happening to someone else and that the doctors or nurses must have made a mistake, or they feel that it is all a nightmare and that they will wake up soon and all will be well. They may also feel very angry.

Rejection is probably less common than might be supposed. In one study only 4% of parents said that they felt rejection.[4] However, only 29% of the parents in this study had been told in the first week after birth, and many were told considerably later. Those who do feel rejection may also feel at the same time that they must protect their poor, helpless baby who has done no wrong and who is suffering because of their own (the parents') guilt.

It is tempting to consider the parents' responses in phases. This has inherent problems because using the word 'phase' suggests a progression towards normality and if the abnormal child survives there may never be normality again for those parents. However, it is a useful way in which to describe parents' responses and Cunningham and Jupp describe four phases.[3]

The first phase is that of shock, numbness and denial. They then move on to a reaction phase where they are attempting to understand the disability and regain control of their lives. The third phase is one of adjustment or adaptation when they are asking 'What can be done?' or 'How can we get help?' At this stage they are beginning to regain their self esteem. The final phase is one of orientation, where they are beginning to establish new routines and life begins to take on a new 'normality' and they appear to have adjusted to their problems and to cope very well.

Parents have to face many difficulties, not least the reactions of the people with whom they come into contact. If their baby is obviously abnormal, then some people approach them in the street or supermarket and ask them what they did wrong—'Did you fall during pregnancy?' or 'Did you drink?' This can be very hurtful. On the other hand, if their abnormal child looks normal then when he knocks over a stack of 600 cans of baked beans in the supermarket, the accusing looks make it clear that they are to blame for having brought him up so badly.

Some parents cope very well while they have normal children as well, but when the normal children grow up and leave the nest, they then have to make family outings with just the abnormal child. The guilt, shame and awfulness may then return and they may no longer cope.

FOLLOW UP

The parents should be seen several times in the hours and days after the disclosure of the diagnosis. It is also vital that the parents are introduced to professionals from the community health services while they are still in hospital, so that they know that they will not be left isolated and without help once they go home. It is helpful for the parents to be able to discuss with them the various agencies and people from whom they can expect help and support.

Parents do not really distinguish between practical and emotional help, they just find who helps them and that is the person that they rely on. They need to know, or be able to find out, who the appropriate person is to turn to for help and to answer their questions.

I believe that the timing and the way in which the parents are told about the problems initially have a profound effect on the way in which they subsequently use the available services. It is clear from Cunningham and others that parental satisfaction is more dependent on the way in which they were told the bad news than on the news itself.[4]

REFERENCES

1 Hogg J, Lamb L, Cowie J, Coxen J. People with profound retardation and multiple handicaps attending schools or social education centres. Mencap

PRMH project report, 1987. Piper Hill School, 200 Yew Tree Lane, Northenden, Manchester M23 0FF.

2 Cunningham C C, Morgan P A, McGucken R B. Down's Syndrome: Is dissatisfaction with disclosure of diagnosis inevitable? *Developmental Medicine and Child Neurology*. 1984;**26**:33–9.

3 Cunningham C C, Jupp S. Early parent counselling—a literature review. In: Parents deserve better—a review report of early counselling in Wales. SCOVO, 32 Tower Bridge Road East, Canton, Cardiff CF1 9DU.

4 Quine L, Pahl J. First diagnosis of severe handicap: A study of parental reactions. *Developmental Medicine and Child Neurology*. 1987;**29**:232–42.

DISCUSSION

Audience You mentioned the value of putting parents in touch with 'experienced parents' who have already had a child with special needs. You pointed out the difficulty of finding another family with a child with exactly the same diagnosis. From my experience of working such a scheme, the value comes often from meeting another parent who has gone through the experience, rather than meeting another parent with a child who has exactly the same diagnosis.

Dr Pearse I agree entirely. The problem is that if the first baby with, for example, Down's Syndrome develops leukaemia, the parents who have been introduced live in fear and foreboding of this happening to their child.

Audience I question the suggestion that the breaking of bad news is best done with only one professional in the room. It may be one of those common sense assumptions where further research is needed. There is fragmentary evidence from a paediatric cardiology unit that parents participated more when there were a number of people in the room, often when bad news was being broken. The ability to avoid direct eye to eye contact with the doctor for periods in the discussion and the opportunity to collect one's thoughts may actually be of use.

Dr Pearse Cliff Cunningham sent questionnaires to parents who had been counselled in various settings with one or more people, and the parents preferred the one to one situation.

Audience Yes, indeed, these patients also preferred the one to one setting, but when tape recordings of the meetings were studied, it was found that the parents participated more when there were more people in the room.

Dr Pearse I find that very surprising as it goes against my experience.

BREAKING BAD NEWS TO CHILDREN IN PAEDIATRIC CARE

Dr G Forrest
Consultant Child Psychiatrist
Park Hospital for Children, Oxford

Learning that you or someone close to you has a serious chronic life-threatening illness is a major stress—perhaps greatest of all if it concerns a child. We know that significant numbers of children with chronic life-threatening illnesses suffer from emotional disorders and how the child first finds out about his condition may well affect his adjustment to what lies ahead. The purpose of this paper therefore is to explore the issues surrounding the breaking of such bad news to children, so that we may be better equipped to handle this in the best possible way.

I would like to start with some theoretical considerations. The life events work of Paykel in adults and Goodyer in children confirms that it is the meaning of the event to the individual that is the most important factor. So what does it mean to a six year old to be told he has cancer? What does he understand of the language and the implication of it? The emotional context surrounding the event is also significant, so for example if a child is with weeping parents and is told that he has some small minor thing wrong with him which is going to be all right in the end, he will not believe it. The message for him is that something very serious and upsetting is happening, and also that you cannot talk about that directly. I am not going to deal with parents' reactions further, except to say that they colour the child's perceptions very greatly and staff need to work closely with parents over breaking of bad news to children.

Communicating anything is much easier if we know the individual well. But with children, it is also vital that we are aware of their level of understanding of the language used. For example Kevin, age 7½, knows he has a tumour in his leg, but doesn't know what that is and feels confused and angry when the doctors say that they therefore will have to take his leg off. Lewis, age 7, whose brother has a Wilm's tumour, has been told that this is a 'bug' and he has spent the year since learning this, waiting, in a state of great anxiety, for the next person in his family to catch the 'bug'. His previous experience of bugs has been of coughs, colds and measles.

The second important aspect of communication with children is an awareness of the developmental stage they are at. Figure 1 illustrates simply the Eriksonian view of personality development, and the impact of illness and the sick role at each of these stages of development, will have different implications and a different meaning for the child.[1] For

Infancy	Pre-school	Schoolchild	Adolescent
Can I trust them?		Can I do it?	
	Will they let me?		Who am I?

Figure 1

example, if we take the under fives, having to accept investigations and treatment, hospitalisations and separation from home and family, is directly opposed to the developmental stage of the child where he is striving to achieve control of himself and his environment. Illness during the primary school years will almost certainly interfere with the child's capacity to develop his mastery of cognitive skills, falling behind in his educational attainments and losing his sense of self-esteem in his prowess at other school-based activities. Serious chronic illness in the adolescent years can be particularly difficult, with many implications for a need to re-define the young person's sense of self and self-esteem in very different ways. For example a 13 year old girl whose self-esteem was rooted in both her personal appearance and her gymnastic ability was faced with the amputation of her leg left with an osteo-sarcoma, and all the changes in appearance that go along with cytotoxic therapy. She responded to this by becoming mute and withdrawn for the first month after her diagnosis was made.

What about the development of children's ability to conceptualise death? The work of Kane in America has contributed to our understanding of the way children build their concept of death.[2] Figure 2 shows the concepts identified in earlier studies which contribute to the

11

COMPONENTS OF THE CONCEPT OF DEATH
(Kane 1979)

Realisation	all	3 year olds
Separation		5 year olds
Immobility		5 year olds
Irrevocability		6 year olds
Causality		6 year olds
Dysfunctionality		6 year olds
Universality		7 year olds
Insensitivity		8 year olds
Appearance		12 year olds

Figure 2

total overall concept of death and the average ages at which these concepts are acquired by children. It is interesting to note that if a child has direct experience of death and dying, it is only if this experience happens before the age of 6 that we see a significant change in the rate of acquisition of the concepts.

Now we can turn to look at the development of the child's concept of serious illness. Bluebond Langner,[3] a social anthropologist, carried out a study of leukaemic children in the States, and discovered through her observation of the children, the way in which they gradually developed their concepts of illness through observation and experience. These are the phases that she identified:

1. I am very sick.
2. I am seriously ill but will get better.
3. I am always ill and will get better.
4. I am always ill and will never get better.
5. I am dying.

Many children never reach stage 5: those who do, reach it after they have directly experienced another child's death from the same illness. Lansdown of Great Ormond Street has produced a similar scheme for the stages of understanding life-threatening illness by children:[4]

1. I am very sick.
2. I have an illness that can kill people.
3. I have an illness that can kill children.
4. I may not get better.
5. I am dying.

12

The important thing about the way in which children develop their understanding of their illness is that it takes time, irrespective of the amount of information that they have been given.

Parents may well be unaware of the stage of understanding that their child has reached. My colleagues, Alan Stein, Helen Woolley, David Baum and myself are carrying out a study of chronically ill children using a hospice in Oxford, and comparing them with a group of children who are not using the hospice. We asked the parents of intellectually intact children what they thought their children knew or understood of their illness. Half the parents said they thought their children had little or no understanding and four-fifths of the children had asked very little or no questions about their illness and its outcome. However, one child with muscular dystrophy had announced at a Christmas lunch that he might not be eating another lunch like that one but 'don't worry I'll be back to haunt you'. A 5 year old who had been critically ill at the age of 3 had recently told his parents, who believed he had little memory of the acute state of illness, that 'I nearly died: I went to heaven to grandad to a castle in the sky. They had lots of toys for me to play with there. But I came back because you didn't want me to go. I will go to grandad another day.' Figure 3 contains a summary of those factors which have shown to be sources of stress for children with chronic life-threatening illnesses. This list includes the symptoms, the treatment and its side-effects, mutilating or body changing experiences, separation from home, reaction of the parents, over-dependence and restriction of freedom.

Now I would like to move on to more practical considerations. Dr Pearse has already talked about the emotional reactions of adults to bad news. In children we see three main features, anger, mourning and guilt: the anger and sadness at the various losses which the child's illness represents to him or her, and the guilt which is a very common component as the child strives to understand why this has happened to him. For example, a child who had developed a tumour on his leg believed that this had happened because he had knocked his leg while sledging some months earlier, when he had been forbidden to go out on his sledge that day. A little 3 year old, learning that her new baby sister whom she had not wanted very much, had died, said, 'What did I do mummy? Hurt the baby so she went away?' In breaking bad news to children therefore we must anticipate these normal reactions, and also be prepared to deal with them.

Children, of course, have their own ways of dealing with their emotional reactions. Geist identifies the following common coping mechanisms in children on paediatric wards. Intellectualisation, when a child seeks to master the event through factual knowledge; identification with the medical staff, denial in the service of hope where denial, a very useful coping strategy, is used in order to sustain the child's cheerful optimistic outlook on life, but not at the expense of co-operating with essential medical procedures and treatments. And lastly, rituals serve

SOURCES OF STRESS FOR CHILD

Age

Symptoms

Treatment and side-effects

Mutilating or body-changing experiences

Separation from home

Reaction of parents

Overdependence

Restriction of freedom

Figure 3

many children well as they strive to cope with repeated painful or unpleasant procedures.

How can we help children facing the onset of chronic illness? Geist again has outlined five ways of doing this. Firstly, unconditionally accepting the whole patient, warts and all, bad temper and all. Secondly, he emphasises the need to present the loss as permanent, if indeed it is so. So the 7 year old facing the amputation of his leg asks if he will grow another one when he is 21. He needs to be told firmly that this will not happen. Similarly, the juvenile onset diabetic child needs to be given an unequivocal answer to the question of whether or not his diabetes will ever get better. Thirdly, Geist emphasises the need for continuity of care by professional staff, and continuity of care at home by the parents, so that the style of family interaction, family rules and limits are kept as close as possible to how they were before the onset of the illness. Lastly, he emphasises the need to create opportunities for children to feel valued in the ward setting, to prevent them from turning to the sick role as the only source of value and self-esteem.

Finally, I would like to mention the siblings of chronically ill children, who show almost as high levels of emotional disorder as the ill children themselves. Again studies have identified the main sources of stress for siblings in this situation and these are shown in Figure 4. I would like to highlight two of these—their ignorance about the illness and feeling 'left out'. Siblings frequently are confused, troubled, ignorant about what is happening to their brother or sister, and particularly older siblings in the adolescent group long to be able to be included in discussions with the medical staff about what is wrong and what is happening to their brother or sister. These surely give us indications of how we may help reduce the sources of stress for siblings caught up in this situation.

14

SOURCES OF STRESS FOR SIBLINGS

Disruption of home life

Ignorance about illness

Feeling 'left out'

Parents' mental state

Guilt over healthiness

Envy of sick child

Reactions of friends—school

Figure 4

To conclude, I would like to quote some golden rules for breaking bad news to children. Firstly, work in close partnership with the parents wherever possible. Secondly, stick as close to the truth as possible. Thirdly, be aware of both the general and the specific implications of the disease for that individual child, and be ready for, and accept, their emotional reactions.

REFERENCES

1 Erikson E. *Childhood and Society* Penguin Books in Association with the Hogarth Press.
2 Kane B. Children's concepts of death *Journal of Genetic Psychology* 1979;**134**:141–53.
3 Bluebond Langer M. *The Private Worlds of Dying Children* N.J. Princeton University Press, 1978.
4 Lansdown R. *More Than Sympathy* London: Tavistock Publications, 1980.

DISCUSSION

Audience Have you any suggestions on how to deal with the parents who wish to protect the child from the diagnosis?

Dr Forrest It is important to try and carry the parents along in whatever you are doing. You need to spend time and use as many strategies as necessary to help parents see the need to share information with the child. I mentioned a girl who had had her leg amputated as an adolescent due to cancer; her parents instructed that it was better for her not to know about the decision to amputate until two days before her surgery. Not enough effort was made to convince those parents that that was not going to be helpful for that girl. It is dangerous to cut across parents in this situation and tell the child yourself, because that seriously interferes not only with your relationship with them, but also it undermines their relationship with their own child. If they are not ready to accept the consequences of that news, they are not ready to deal with it themselves.

Audience Would you recommend the technique of asking the child what he thinks is wrong with him or herself in front of the parents? The children often know.

Dr Forrest Yes, if you are sure that the child does know and it is a question of getting it all out into the open, that can be a good way. I'd like to say a little more about siblings. Much interest has directed towards the plight of siblings who are caught up in the situation of having a brother or sister with a life-threatening illness. Many siblings, particularly the adolescents, feel they never have the opportunity to understand truthfully what is happening; they are given a 'watered-down' version from their parents when they feel they want to know more and they want to understand fully. Younger children do not put that into words so well, but they too complain of being confused. It is an area where we could do a lot more by helping the siblings of these children understand what is going on and why.

FAMILY SUPPORT AFTER COT-DEATH

Dr Jonathan Couriel MA MRCP
Consultant in Paediatrics
and Paediatric Respiratory Medicine
Booth Hall Children's Hospital, Manchester

Give sorrow words: the grief that does not speak
Whispers the o'er-fraught heart, and bids it break.
Macbeth, Act IV, Scene 3

Over 1500 infants die suddenly and unexpectedly in England and Wales each year, an incidence of 1 in 450 live-births.[1] Such cot-deaths are the commonest cause of death in children aged between one week and one year.[2] In 80% of these cot-deaths, a thorough post-mortem examination fails to establish an adequate explanation for why the child has died and they are classified as the Sudden Infant Death Syndrome (SIDS). In the remaining minority, the post-mortem reveals an unsuspected cause of death, such as pneumonia or, less commonly, a congenital anomaly.[2]

Over the last twenty years, there has been a great deal of research to establish the cause of SIDS. Although this research has increased our understanding of normal and abnormal physiological processes in infancy and allowed us to recognise some risk factors for some cot-deaths, and although many hypotheses have been proposed, the aetiology of most cases of SIDS remains unknown. Research has led to the conclusion that there is no single cause of sudden infant death: SIDS is not a discrete entity, simply a common end-point for several pathological processes.

Less attention has been paid to the effects of a sudden infant death on the family, and the ways in which doctors and other health professionals can best help such families.[3,4,5] Much of the impetus to recognise and meet the needs of bereaved parents has not come from professionals, but from parent support groups, notably the Foundation for the Study of Infant Deaths in London.[6,7] The Foundation not only provides support and advice for bereaved families (and professionals) but can put families in touch with local support groups or 'befrienders'. (It also funds much of the medical research done on SIDS.)

In the last five years, the British Paediatric Association, in recognition of the emotional impact of a cot-death on a family, has recommended that each health district should have a nominated consultant paediatrician who is prepared to offer support and counselling to families who have lost a baby in this way. In this paper I would like to present my experience over the last four years of providing such paediatric support to 54 families who have suffered a cot-death, to describe some of the lessons I have learnt during the evolution of this service, and to make suggestions of how such support and counselling for these families can best be co-ordinated.

SOURCE OF REFERRALS

Parents have been referred to me from a number of different sources. Nineteen families were referred by the Foundation for the Study of Infant Deaths. In North Manchester, the obstetricians and midwives inform me of women booking into the local ante-natal clinics who have lost a previous child from cot-death, and there have been 14 referrals from this source. There have been 7 families referred by general practitioners or health visitors, 6 from Accident and Emergency departments and 4 from paediatricians. Four families referred themselves after publicity in the local press about the service provided at Booth Hall.

A striking feature of many referrals has been the lack of support that families have received from any health professional, and their resentment or anger about this. The interval between the death of the child and my first contact with the family has varied from hours to 12 years. Overall, the number of visits by each family varied from 1 to 14: 20 families had more than 6 sessions. I have had 237 consultations with these families in total.

IMPACT ON THE FAMILY

The loss of any child inevitably has profound effects on surviving members of the family: this family can never be the same again. However, cot-deaths differ from other childhood deaths in two critical respects which profoundly affect the reactions of the parents. These are the suddenness of the death, and, most importantly, the lack of any explanation of the death.[8]

If a child dies from a severe infection or a malignancy, the family will have some time, even if it is only a brief period of illness before the death, in which to prepare themselves. With a cot-death, the absence of any warning of the impending tragedy increases the sense of disbelief which naturally follows the death of a child—'He can't be dead: I fed him only an hour ago and he was perfectly all right.' The absence of any explanation of why the child has died increases this disbelief and prevents parents from exonerating themselves of their guilt—'we must have done something wrong—a healthy baby doesn't die for no reason at all.' One can believe that one's child has died from a road traffic accident or from pneumonia, but it is much more difficult to accept a death for which there is no apparent explanation. Many parents find it difficult to believe that we doctors, with all our knowledge and technology, in most cases of cot-

18

death can offer no explanation for why their baby has died. The parents' guilt is also increased by the unavoidable involvement of the police and coroner, and often by the reactions of relatives and friends.

Some authors have described a sequence of stages or phases in the grieving process. Classically there is disbelief or denial, followed by anger, guilt or blame. Later there is depression and apathy, followed eventually by resignation and acceptance. Whilst this is a useful framework for working with bereaved parents, it is a mistake to believe that all parents grieve in the same sequence of stages, or that once one stage has been left that those feelings cannot return at a later time, often in response to some external event.

It is important to realise that a cot-death affects the whole family, not only the mother and father, but brothers and sisters, grandparents and other relatives and friends. In some cases, such a tragedy brings members of a family closer together. Unfortunately, in a number of families I have seen, the grief has pushed people apart. Grief often reduces our ability to care for and support the people closest to us when they need us most.

'Their sorrows were separate, insular, incommunicable. They went their different ways, he with his lists and trudging, she in her armchair, lost in deep private grief. They huddled over their separate losses, and unspoken resentments began to grow.'
Ian McEwan, *The Child in Time*.

Different members of the family grieve in different ways. They also receive support in different ways. Society has a hierarchy of sympathy. After a cot-death, most of the attention is directed to the mother. It is expected that it will be the father who will register the death, who will arrange the funeral and contact the relatives. He is often expected to return to work after a few days or a couple of weeks—'He should be getting over it by now: it'll do no good sitting at home moping.' In my experience, it is unusual for anyone to sit down with the father, to let him talk, to let him cry. These circumstances make it very difficult to persuade men to express their feelings. Many men feel that they must be strong, that it is unacceptable weakness to show their sorrow. Some fathers express themselves in very dramatic ways: four fathers have simply walked out on the family and have not returned. Some men drink excessively, others 'bury' themselves in their work. These are all methods of escaping from facing up to one's feelings. Denial by fathers and by mothers can be very powerful: many parents have told me that they did not really believe that their baby was dead until the funeral.

In two-thirds of families who lose a baby from cot-death there are other children. The needs of surviving siblings are often overlooked, by other family members and by the supporting agencies. Often these other children will have been present when the baby has been discovered to be dead: not infrequently they will have been the one who tried to wake up their little brother or sister before they realised that something was terribly wrong. They will almost certainly have witnessed the horrified reaction of their parents and their frantic attempts at resuscitation. They are often shunted away to be looked after by friends or relatives, which, although understandable, inevitably increases their confusion and insecurity.

After a cot-death, most siblings regress, both physically and emotionally: enuresis, stammering and clinging to mummy are very common. Some children become very angry with their parents—'Why did you send the baby away: are you going to send me away too?' Acting out the discovery of the baby's body or the funeral are extremely distressing for parents. Many siblings worry that they may have been responsible for the death because they had 'bad thinks' about their brother or sister, so-called 'magical thinking'. Sometimes the child adopts the role of the comforter in the family. In older children, problems with school performance and relations with peers are common for months or one or two years after the death.[10,11,12]

PROVIDING SUPPORT

How can the paediatrician, and the other health professionals who come into contact with the bereaved family, help? I find it useful to divide the timing of professional support into three fairly arbitrary phases.

Immediate Phase

In the first few days after the death, and sometimes for as long as one or two weeks after the funeral, most parents are so shocked, so numb and so confused that attempts to talk about their feelings are unlikely to be productive and for some, may be more of an imposition than a help. What most parents need is a prompt, simple and sympathetic explanation that it appears that their child has died from a cot-death but that a post-mortem will be needed to confirm this.

It is very important that parents are given an opportunity to 'say goodbye' to their baby. We always encourage mothers and fathers to hold and cuddle their dead child. A quiet room, away from the bustle and commotion of the casualty department, where they can have privacy and time is needed. Any sense of rushing the parents must be avoided. Other members of the family, such as grandparents or occasionally older siblings of the dead child, may want to see him for the last time. Quite frequently parents want to see the baby again perhaps one or two days after the death and arrangements should be made so this is possible. Failure to provide this special time can lead to long-term problems later on which may be difficult to rectify.

The involvement of the police and the coroner (both of whom must be informed), and the fact that a post-mortem is mandatory because the cause of death is unknown, also need to be explained sympathetically.

Parents should be warned that the police will wish to interview them and that they usually visit the scene of death and remove bedding or other items which they regard as evidence. The parents can be told that it is unusual for there to be an inquest after a cot-death, but this decision will be made by the coroner after the post-mortem. They also need practical advice about registering the child's death and arranging the funeral. There are other practicalities to be considered: if the mother has been breast-feeding she should be prescribed bromocriptine to suppress lactation.

The paediatrician has an important role in co-ordinating communication after a child has been brought into hospital dead. There is a long list of people who need to be informed (Table 1), and failure to contact them soon after the death results in embarrassing and distressing gaffs. The general practitioner and the health visitor should be telephoned as soon as possible after the death. The community midwife and the local child-health also need to be informed. In this era of computerised invitations for immunisations or hearing checks, someone has to tell the computer that the child has died. We have found the early involvement of a medical social worker to be of great value; many will have special skills in bereavement counselling. Depending on the parents' wishes, it may be helpful to contact a minister of religion. We offer to contact relatives or friends for the parents and ensure that they do not return home alone: often our social worker will offer to accompany them home. The parents can be offered a visit from the local cot-death support group, although in my experience, this is often more appropriate at a later stage. We give parents an excellent pamphlet produced by the Foundation for the Study of Infant Deaths which gives useful information and advice.

Being involved with a cot-death is also distressing for nursing and medical staff, and for the ambulance crew, who are likely to have attempted resuscitation. The paediatrician can ensure that this stress is recognised and discussed.

It will be clear that there are quite a number of tasks which need to be done and that it is all too easy for at least one to be forgotten: for this reason we have been using a simple check-list to ensure that such errors of omission are avoided (Table 2).

TABLE 1   Agencies involved with the family after a cot-death

General Practitioner	Health Visitor
Ambulance Staff	Paediatrician
Police	Social Worker
Coroner	Local Child Health Clinic
Pathologist	Minister of Religion
Funeral Director	SIDS support group
Accident and Emergency Staff	Community Midwife

TABLE 2   Booth Hall Children's Hospital checklist for sudden infant
deaths

Child's Name . . . .
Date of birth. . . . .   Date of death. . . . .

1. Registrar or Consultant spoken to parents   . . . .
2. Brief clinical history taken   . . . .
3. Examination/investigations done   . . . .
4. Parents offered to be with/hold baby   . . . .
5. Police and coroner informed   . . . .
6. Medical social worker informed   . . . .
7. GP informed   . . . .
8. Health visitor informed   . . . .
9. Minister of religion informed   . . . .
10. Advice on registration and funeral given   . . . .
11. Pamphlet from SIDS Foundation given   . . . .
12. Phone number of local Friends of SIDS given   . . . .
13. Consultant follow-up arranged   . . . .
14. Social worker follow-up arranged   . . . .
15. Community physician informed   . . . .

Intermediate Phase

It used to be suggested that the correct time to see the bereaved family to
discuss the post-mortem results death was about 6 weeks after the death.
I have found this is too long a period for them to wait and I now normally
arrange to see them after two or three weeks (our pathologist phones the
result of the post-mortem to the GP who will usually go to explain the
results to the parents). I find it quite helpful to have a semi-structured
approach to this interview (Table 3), which normally lasts between one
and one and a half hours. A busy out-patient clinic is an inappropriate
setting and I see parents in a quiet office.

There is often an uneasy silence at the beginning of this meeting. I start
by introducing myself and explaining why I have arranged the meeting
and by commenting that I know that it is often very difficult and painful
for them to come to the hospital. Rather than immediately trying to
discuss their feelings, I start by suggesting that many parents in their
situation find it helpful for me to explain the results of the post-mortem.
It is difficult to overemphasise the importance of these results to parents.
A major complaint of parents in a survey done by the SIDS Foundation
was that either the post-mortem results had never been explained or that
there was an unacceptable delay.

After going through these results, I ask for brief details of the
pregnancy, delivery and neonatal period. Had the parents had any

22

TABLE 3   Semi-structured interview

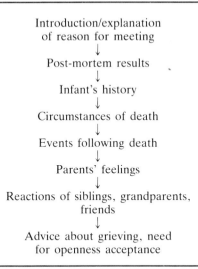

Introduction/explanation
of reason for meeting
↓
Post-mortem results
↓
Infant's history
↓
Circumstances of death
↓
Events following death
↓
Parents' feelings
↓
Reactions of siblings, grandparents,
friends
↓
Advice about grieving, need
for openness acceptance

worries about the child before he died or had he been perfectly well? Was there anything different about him on the day he died? These questions almost always lead into a harrowing description of the discovery of the dead child, the frantic efforts at resuscitation, the dash to the hospital in the ambulance and then to be told that their child was dead. Although discussion of these events is inevitably upsetting, it is unavoidable if there is to be a useful interchange. At this point it is appropriate to start to discuss how they are feeling now, and about how friends and relatives have reacted.

The intense feeling of guilt that most parents experience needs to be discussed early on in the interview. Often this centres around some objectively trivial or irrelevant action—'I shouldn't have taken her to the shops', or, 'I had never closed her bedroom door before.' It is often relatively easy to banish this idea, although frequently it is immediately replaced by another equally illogical but equally distressing notion. As I have mentioned earlier, the absence of a rational explanation of the death encourages the propagation of these sorts of ideas. I ask parents if they feel angry at all, and if so with whom—themselves, each other, the baby for doing this to them? Again many parents feel that anger is inappropriate in this situation and they are reassured to hear it is a common and normal part of grieving.

There is almost universal underestimation of how long it takes to 'get over it'. Many parents become angry with themselves after only a few weeks because they are still weeping, are still unable to look at other children without becoming very upset. I explain to them that it is an unrealistic belief that they should be able to cope with their feelings after such a short period and that we know that it usually takes months or perhaps even one or two years before they can reach that point where they can think about their baby without 'falling apart'.

If there are other children I ask how they have reacted and how they are behaving. The parents often need advice about what they should tell surviving siblings about the death of the child. This very much depends on their age child which, as Dr Forrest has so clearly described, governs the child's understanding of death. I advise them to be honest rather than giving euphemistic explanations. It is better to say 'James was very ill and he died and he won't be able to come back to us' rather than saying 'James is up in the sky' or 'the angels came and took him when he was asleep'. I think it is best if parents can talk to their children themselves rather than the paediatrician doing this. Although I have done this on a number of occasions, I am not sure how helpful it has been. There may be problems with the parents' interaction with surviving siblings or, later on, with subsequent siblings.

Many parents fear that they are going insane. It is common for them to have hallucinations such as hearing the baby cry or imagining that they see the baby's face in another child and they need reassurance that this is a normal reaction.

Some parents start thinking about having another baby very soon after a cot-death, although in my experience, it is uncommon for them to regard this as a replacement child. Most parents understand that each child is a unique, irreplaceable individual. I explain that for both physical and psychological reasons, it is wise to wait for at least six or twelve months before embarking on another pregnancy, but that the final decision really must be theirs. I explain that we recognise that pregnancy is a stressful time and that we are willing to offer them support both before and after the birth of a new baby.

Some parents ask whether they will ever be happy again. I reassure them that this will happen. It may be helpful at this point for them to meet parents from the Friends of the SIDS Foundation who have been through similar experiences.

I ask about the reactions of other relatives and friends. Often friends have been a wonderful comfort but, not infrequently, thoughtless comments from friends can cause great resentment or upset for the parents. I sometimes see myself as a sort of paediatric ACAS trying to explain the other person's point of view. I may say to parents, 'Well just try and imagine yourself in your friend's situation. How would you react?' I explain that it is often very difficult to know what to say to a close friend who has just lost a baby.

Marital conflict is quite common. Again I see myself as trying to explain that men and women react in different ways to a death and that couples have to learn to accept these differences. Many parents cannot face being in the house where the death occurred and over 50% move within twelve months of the death. A number of men have been unable to continue their work because of poor concentration and depression and this loss of employment has been an added burden for the family. One father has attempted suicide but fortunately was unsuccessful.

There have been several very difficult psychiatric problems that I have seen in families after a cot-death. One mother needed admission to a psychiatric unit because of incapacitating anxiety and panic attacks. One father developed an obsession with his health and severe hypochondriasis so that he became unable to carry on his profession. With one family, recurrent apnoeic attacks in a subsequent sibling following a genuine cot-death were eventually proven to be caused by the mother partially smothering the child with her hand, an example of the Munchausen by proxy syndrome. In this case the child needed to be removed from the family and to be made a Ward of Court. In another situation there was a bizarre re-enactment of the circumstances which had led to the previous child's death when the new child was born. In all these situations I enlisted the involvement of an adult psychiatrist after discussion with the parents' GP. It is interesting to note that in all of these pathological responses to a cot-death, there had been major psychological problems in the affected parent long before the cot-death occurred. I have learnt from bitter experience that the 'premorbid personality', and previous experience of a death in the family are very important in determining the reactions of parents to a cot-death. Looking at the circumstances around the time of the death is not sufficient.[13]

The parents will often have questions about what we know about cot-death. Many will have read books or articles about the subject. Invariably, they will ask about the risk of recurrence with future children. A common source of confusion and worry is the relationship between cot-death and the Sudden Infant Death Syndrome. They may have been told by one doctor that their baby died from SIDS and by another that their baby was a cot-death. I explain that the term cot-death simply describes a sudden and unexpected death of an infant, whereas the term SIDS is reserved for those cot-deaths where the post-mortem is either entirely normal or where any detected abnormality is insufficient to explain the death; in other words, SIDS is a sub-group of the cot-death population.

At the end of this interview it may be evident that there are still a number of issues which need to be resolved. I usually offer to see the parents on a different occasion after 2 or 3 weeks. I am very much guided by the parents' response in deciding on how many sessions are required. Initially I thought one session was sufficient but I now believe that this is rarely the case.

Long-term Support

Parents have requested further meetings because they have specific questions or unresolved dilemmas many months or years after the death. It is well recognised that future pregnancies are associated with great anxiety and the reopening of old wounds after a cot-death. For this reason I am referred all women from the antenatal clinic who have lost a previous child from cot-death or sudden death of any cause. I normally see these parents two or three times in the antenatal period and soon after the delivery of the new baby. It is important to have an opportunity to discuss unresolved grief early on in the pregnancy, and to then move on to developing a positive feeling about the new baby, rather than seeing the parents just before or, even worse, just after the birth of the next baby. I then review the infant regularly every 3–6 weeks, depending on the wishes of the family.

This sort of support has been very successful. It works best when it is co-ordinated with support in the community from the family doctor, the health visitor and a social worker. Some parents will want respiration monitors ('apnoea alarms') when the new baby is born. If so, I explain the advantages and disadvantages of using these and ensure that the correct use and simple resuscitation is demonstrated if they are loaned out from the hospital. If this sort of service is to be provided for subsequent siblings then flexibility and accessibility to the hospital are essential.

SUMMARY

The paediatrician has four important tasks in providing support of families who have lost a baby from cot-death. Giving the parents an opportunity to talk openly about their feelings and to ask questions about cot-death is of vital importance. There is a need for co-ordination of all the caring agencies that are involved after a cot-death and this can be most easily organised from the paediatric department. There is a need for somebody within each District or Region to have special experience and knowledge of cot-death who can be contacted by general practitioners or health visitors to give advice about parents' problems. Finally, an important function of the paediatrician is education. How we are going to impart an understanding of the problems faced by bereaved families to doctors in training, to medical students and to other people who work in the health services? Until we answer this last question, there are likely to be continuing deficiencies in the support these families receive and which they so clearly deserve.

REFERENCES

1 Office of Population, Censuses and Surveys. Infant Mortality. London, HMSO, 1988.
2 Arneil G C, Gibson A A M, McIntosh H *et al*. National post-perinatal infant mortality and cot-death study, Scotland 1981–2. *Lancet* 1985;**i**:740–3.
3 Couriel J M. Helping the cot-death family. Update 1988;**36**:2273–80.
4 Woodward S, Pope A, Robson W J, Hagan O. Bereavement counselling after sudden infant death. *Br Med J* 1985;**290**:363–5.
5 Emery J L. Welfare of families of infants found unexpectedly dead ('Cot-deaths'). *Br Med J* 1972:**i**:612–15.
6 Limerick S. Sudden unexpected infant death: paediatric counselling. *Arch Dis Child* 1983;**58**:467-71.
7 Golding J, Limerick S, Macfarlane A. *Sudden Infant Death: patterns, puzzles and problems*. Shepton Mallet: Open Books Publishing, 1985.
6 Cornwell J, Nurcombe B, Stevens L. Family response to the death of a child by sudden infant death syndrome. *Med J Aust* 1977;**i**:656–8.
8 Harman W V. Death of my baby. *Br Med J* 1981;**282**:35–7.
9 McEwan I. *The child in time*. London, Picador, 1988.
10 Williams M L. Sibling reaction to cot death. *Med J Aust* 1981;**2**:227–31.
11 Pettle M S A, Lansdown R G. Adjustments to the death of a sibling. *Arch Dis Child* 1986;**61**:278–83.
12 Mandell F, McAnulty E H, Carlson A. Unexpected death of an infant sibling. *Pediatrics* 1983;**72**:652–7.
13 Bluglass K. Psychosocial aspects of the sudden infant death syndrome ('cot-death'). J Child *Psychol Psychiatr* 1981;**4**:411–21.

DISCUSSION

Audience   What advice would you give a mother whom you visit for counselling three to six weeks after a cot-death and who turns round and asks you 'If I conceive again, what are the chances of my having another cot-death?'

Dr Couriel   There is some disagreement about the precise recurrence risk for cot-death. I think that the general view now is that the risk is increased by a factor of about two for families who have lost one child from cot-death. The most pessimistic view is that the risk is increased five-fold, to around one in a hundred, but I think that is unnecessarily pessimistic. Occasionally, there will be more than one sudden unexpected death in a family: in that situation it is necessary to consider the possibility of an inherited disorder, or whether there is any suggestion of child abuse as the cause of death. I must stress that I think that these are both unusual situations. In general though, I tell parents who are planning to embark on another pregnancy that the risk is double that of the rest of the population, where the risk is one in 450.

Dr Pearse   I enjoyed your talk very much. One of the things I use as a

27

technique in interviews is just to say to the parents 'How are you?' and you get a lot of information that way. The father often says fine and you then know what sort of a chap he is and how he is dealing with it and that you will have to break that down. If they say 'Fine' I always say 'I don't believe you'. Then you get the barriers down and you can talk about what really matters. I have found this a useful technique. It does work.

Dr Couriel If the father is sitting there silently, saying nothing, then I would point this out and say that many men find it very difficult to talk about their feelings. However, I have to say that I often fail miserably to persuade fathers to open up about their emotions. Sometimes only the mother will come to a meeting, although both parents are always invited. There are obviously many reasons why a father may not be able to come, but in many cases it is clear that it is because of a reluctance to have any discussion with anyone about how he is feeling, about how he is coping.

Dr Pearse What I have done on occasions when the father has not come, is to phone him up. You can have quite an in-depth chat on the phone. I do not like doing this because you cannot see his reactions, but it is better than nothing.

The other thing I have done is to offer to see the father separately. Then he may tell you what he really feels. I have started doing that.

Dr Couriel I have started offering to see fathers separately as well.

The other aspect of the consultation that needs considering is whether these meetings should be taking place in hospital, or whether it may be better to go to the parents' home. Certainly if the baby has been brought to the hospital at the time of death, then returning to the place may present another barrier for them, with the risk of reawakening all those awful memories. However, many parents really want to, and I suspect need to, return to the hospital and find it therapeutic to do so.

Prof Harris It is only fair that I offer Dr Forrest the chance to either rebut or agree with this final point.

Dr Forrest From my own experience of working with parents after perinatal death, I actually believe very strongly that it is important for them to break down this feeling of tremendous antipathy about returning to the hospital, because they are going to need that hospital sooner or later, and I think that as in any phobic situation, it is better to deal with these feelings sooner rather than later.

HIV COUNSELLING:
THE THERAPEUTIC CONTRACT

Timothy M G Acton BSC Dip Clin Psychol
Senior Clinical Psychologist

Breaking the Bad News in this context is the process which commences with a pronouncement to the person sitting in front of you, that they have blood which has tested positive for antibodies to the Human Immuno-deficiency Virus (HIV). It is possible that this same individual will have more Bad News at some stage in the future, that, for example, they have been found to have *pneumocystis pneumonia*: it is a process, and not a discrete event. The initial news is given directly, along the lines, 'We have the result of your blood test for antibodies to HIV, and I'm afraid it's positive.' Of course most people will have had *some* preparation for this news as a result of the requirement that all people considering having this test undergo Pre-test Counselling. Nevertheless, the implications of the news are enormous, and it is almost always a great shock.

The Therapeutic Contract discussed here denotes a relationship whose connotations are widely understood to be related to the practice of counselling therapies. This is not exclusively so, indeed a more accurate interpretation would embrace most professions which have direct face-to-face contact with people suffering physical or emotional problems. Indeed in the context of HIV at least, the recognition that the physical and psychological aspects of illness cannot be considered separately is an important ingredient of the Therapeutic Contract.

For the sake of convenience, I will define the frame of reference as comprising four distinct areas: Confidentiality, Access, Consistency, and Understanding. The aim is to consider the vital contribution of each of these factors in the Health Care system for persons who carry HIV, and that any 'contract' which exists in the absence of any of these factors is diminished accordingly.

Confidentiality

At the most explicit level, an Act of Parliament exists which serves to protect individuals attending departments of Genitourinary Medicine from inappropriate or unconsented disclosure of details of their medical case histories to others. Confidentiality is also implicit in the counselling relationship, whereby for individuals to be able to modify their behaviour, or work through their feelings about a diagnosis and its implications, it is important for them to trust their doctors and counsellors, and raise the issue of what will and what will not, what can

29

and what cannot, be disclosed. Confidentiality has implications where family, lovers and others may wish to seek support from the same worker, which can entail the possibility of compromising the client and the professional, and attenuate trust. The power of this rule has unfortunately been attested on the occasions when it has been broken, leading to lost jobs, ostracisation and rejection by families and friends. Thoughts of appeal to the forum of public tribunals, in the cases of those who have lost jobs, are tempered by the sure knowledge that it will lead to more publicity, self-identification as 'the person with AIDS', and so forth. Equally, it is important to encourage these patients to respect their own right to confidentiality: to inform others at the right time for them.

Access

This means being as available as possible within the particular constraints of a given service, with a virus whose manifestations can be sudden and unpredictable. It means accessibility to appropriate health care systems where referral to other departments is indicated, and thus depends on good communication. It means accessibility to information, if requested, concerning appropriate treatments, alternative treatments, and what a given research finding means. It means accessibility, as far as possible, to physicians and counsellors of different genders, to allow for the not uncommon difficulty of some people disclosing personal information to professionals of the opposite sex.

Consistency

Within the therapeutic contract this is closely related to good interdisciplinary liaison and training. The consequences of HIV infection include the potential for manifold symptom expression, and subsequent behavioural and emotional reactions to these, or to the perceived and anticipated threat of these. It is therefore likely that the person who does manifest symptoms to HIV infection will come across a broad spectrum of professionals—general and specialist physicians, nurses, clinical psychologists, social workers, dieticians, and others. The possibilities for confusion that can arise as a result of conflicting or inconsistent information are plentiful. The result is a poor service, distress on the part of the patient, and low compliance with treatments and advice offered. There is a clear need for good understanding of the basic psychosocial, virological and immunological aspects of HIV, and recent research findings. There is a clear need for effective, regular inter-professional communication (e.g. psychologist to social worker, general physician to psychiatrist) and intra-departmental communication (e.g. academic department to NHS department, and outpatient to inpatient departments), and for newcomers to become thoroughly familiar with the set-up and key individuals prior to becoming engaged in direct contact with the patient group.

Understanding

This refers to the whole scenario of both the helper and the helped. It refers, of course, to the process of verbal and non-verbal communication transacted between the participants in this context. The understanding also involves how much both parties know about the patient's diagnosis and prognosis. For example, it involves the portrayal of HIV by the media and its associations with Contagion, Death, and Homosexuality, and the marketable confusion of issues seen in headlines such as 'AIDS MAN BITES TWO COPS'. It means the health care workers examine themselves and their attitudes and feelings toward their clients, and the issues which they will face.

The understanding of the therapeutic contract incorporates acknowledging the psychological processes related to the threat of developing debilitating illnesses, in relation to currently available information. At the beginning it is the information that you are HIV antibody positive. What does this mean? It means exposure to the virus and the development of antibodies to it. It means not being able to say who will develop symptoms, or how to confer protection on asymptomatic carriers of HIV pending results of research into these questions. What we do know is that there is a certain amount of uncertainty and that it can be utterly immobilising. The uncertainties can be lived with, with help: with clear information, where possible, to replace conjecture; with support to alleviate isolation; and with hope to allay fear.

People who are HIV antibody positive do go on to develop symptoms, and numerous questions then arise. Are they treatable? Will I have to tell others? Will I be able to work? There are a whole host of issues heir to the development of physical symptoms with which I am sure the reader is familiar and which, to take just two examples, impinge on understanding of the Therapeutic Contract.

Life Span Development Psychology extends traditional assumptions which account for differences in human development in terms of age-related biological and socialisation processes. Life is understood as a continual process of development where childhood and adolescence are preparatory stages for adulthood—characterised by a period of generativity—and old age is a period of review. Death is part of this process and is concerned with a number of developmental objectives including adaptation to mortality, adaptation to the process of physical decline, adaptation to changing social environments as a result of the loss of significant others, and the task of life review. These themes of the dying process are properly identified as developmental phenomena, exhibit regularity, and are usually based on antecedent history and expectations, and an adaptive social context. The social and medical aspects of HIV often means that

31

this process does not exhibit regularity, and takes place in the absence of well established and well understood antecedent history. For example, the manifestation of debilitating symptomatology at the most productive time of an individual's development can be relatively sudden; and, significant numbers of others may well not be aware of the illness until the last moment, when it brings with it considerations with respect to sexuality and lifestyle which may not be well understood. The therapeutic contract acknowledges this difficulty explicitly in assisting people to work through the desynchrony between developmental processes.

The other feature of HIV-related illnesses and the threat of such concerns the importance of occupational status and unemployment. There is much work on the stress of unemployment, and to take one example, on its deleterious influence on the efficiency of thinking:[1]

> Stress and cognitive performance have often been linked in the literature, using arousal and attention as central concepts, with both under- and over-arousal thought to be productive of performance degradation. Unemployment may plausibly be hypothesised to be stressful in both senses: under-arousing because of low demand characteristics in the absence of employment compulsion and work traction, and over-arousing because of the need to confront unusual problems and unpalatable options.

This effect is therefore superimposed on those mentioned thus far. There is an additional point concerning productivity and work. It could be argued that we live in a society which does not acknowledge the unproductive. The celebration of life is a celebration of how productive an individual is or can be. Many people who become unable to work themselves share this view and suffer the subsequent impact on their self-esteem. The therapeutic contract compensates to some extent for the peripheral importance of birth and dying in a society that is predominantly materialistic, by acknowledging it.

Thus far, this account of the therapeutic contract has acknowledged the foregoing effects related to illness *per se*, and to HIV in particular. It is apposite to give due consideration to the needs of the majority of people who are currently known to be HIV seropositive, i.e. homosexual men. At present, the vast majority of people with AIDS are homosexual men, and it is more than likely that at the moment, and in the immediate future, most people seeking psychological support and medical help as a result of HIV will be homosexual men. It is important to understand why this is important.

The undesirable physical and emotional concomitances of HIV are surely exacerbated when public identification as being a person with AIDS, or person carrying HIV, gives permission for individual and collective expressions of disapproval. Since 1967 the legal injunctions against men expressing themselves sexually to other men have been lifted somewhat: society sanctions a degree of tolerance of homosexuals, so long as they do not want to adopt children, hold public office, express themselves physically in public, and so on. Most people will acknowledge that there is a history of anti-homosexuality in this country, whether or not they condemn or condone it.

To be male and HIV seropositive at the moment means to be identified as homosexual, and to be open to prevailing attitudes toward homosexuality (often hostile), rather than prevailing attitudes to illness (often caring and compassionate). The therapeutic contract recognises this overlay, and its effect.

It means that the threat of the emergence of physical symptomatology is doubly anxiety provoking: it brings with it the possibility of pain, the implication of viral activity, and the signal to others that all is not well: that it is no longer possible to cover up disfiguring symptomatology and the association with a marginalised social group.

CONCLUSION

This text has served as an introduction to the idea of the therapeutic contract in HIV counselling. The *access, confidentiality, consistency,* and *understanding* are present in varying degrees, and in direct proportion to the efficacy of the therapeutic relationship.

Finally, the therapeutic contract is an affirmation of a joint enterprise undertaken by equals: it is consumer oriented: it includes the individual patient, and their partners, families, and friends, making use of a resource according to need, and often in a challenging way. There is, of course, still room for the sick role, and illness behaviour, but the well observed strictures of the expert doctor/passive patient apply less and less.

Within this overall scheme of things, individuals develop symptoms and allow the temporary relinquishment of their autonomy by, for example, being medically investigated, or working through being depressed, and focus on specific issues, such as for example:

the perception of the loss of control following hospitalisation;
the fear of a painful and lonely death;
what, how, and when to tell others, especially parents; and,
how to support lovers.

The actual wording of the contract is unimportant, what is important is that it can be written at all, and in order to be able to do this, it is necessary for professionals in face-to-face contact with these individuals to work out their part of the contract over and above the application of sound clinical skills, and in a manner which will facilitate their uptake.

REFERENCE

1 Unemployment and cognitive difficulties. David Fryer and Peter Warr *British Journal of Clinical Psychology* 1984;**23**:63–8.

FURTHER READING

Life Span Development Psychology. P B Baltes, H W Reese, and L P Lipsitt. *Annual Review of Psychology*. 1980;**31**:65–110.
David Miller *Living with AIDS and HIV*. Macmillan 1987.

IMPARTING THE DIAGNOSIS OF AIDS AND SETTING UP A MODEL OF CARE

Anthony J Pinching
Senior Lecturer in Clinical Immunology
St Mary's Hospital Medical School, London

During this decade physicians from diverse specialities and backgrounds have been drawn together by the needs of a new patient group with the devastating new clinical challenge of AIDS. The physicians have been characterised by a willingness to respond to this challenge, which could have been seen as a threat both to them and their style of clinical practice, and to adapt their skills and approach to suit both the disease and the social milieu in which it occurred. While the specifics of the care models in different settings have varied, many clinicians have moved, consciously or unconsciously, to strategies for care that have more similarities than differences.

An important consequence of the youth of the client group has been that physicians and others have been confronted by the expectations and aspirations of a wholly younger generation than that typically needing care before AIDS. This has demanded an abrupt move from the old and outmoded world of physicianly paternalism to a new one where patients explicitly control their own destinies and where physicians advise and explain, but are clearly servants of the patient. Such a transition in clinical philosophy is clearly timely and appropriate, not only for this disease but for many others.

The clinicians who initially became involved in AIDS care were self-selecting enthusiasts who were keen to learn. They soon found that, while they could carry many colleagues forward with them, there were others whose unwillingness or inability to adapt to the necessarily changed circumstances of AIDS could only be counterproductive. It was not a question of allowing them to exclude themselves from the work, but rather a sense that to force their involvement could jeopardise the care model, to the inevitable detriment of the patient. This was best encapsulated by Dr Connie Wofsy of San Francisco who defined an AIDS specialist as 'someone who has satisfactorily cared for five people with AIDS and is willing to care for more.'

Some of the strengths of the systems that have evolved to date emerged from a type of 'siege mentality' affecting the pioneers. This included taking a role in pressing for the development of appropriate public policy and for new funding for the new epidemic and its control. Advocacy by individuals, community-based groups and by physicians was an over-whelming necessity, which was inevitably first recognised by those in the front-line.

The creation of an ethos of care common to all members of the care team is crucial. It initially emerged from the attitudes of a few key staff and, most importantly, from responses to the patients' views and constructive criticisms. Openness and honesty between patient and health care worker are the hallmarks, with dialogue and true consultation the means of realising an agreed approach to clinical management, where the patient explicitly retains control over clinical decisions. Similarly, complete confidentiality must be assured, thus removing any potential constraints on the professional relationship and ensuring that the patient also explicitly retains control over information about him/herself.

Defining and articulating the professional contract is best done at an early stage, usually when a diagnosis is being considered or has been made. Such early discussions must cover a number of key issues. The nature of AIDS and of HIV must be explained so that the patient understands what immune deficiency means—i.e. susceptibility to a particular range of infections—and that in the case of HIV there is damage to a part of the immune defence system. The important words are 'damage', not destruction, so the patient knows that one of the objectives is to make the best of what remains, and 'part' since they should understand that some parts of immune defence remain intact and that they will handle many infections normally. The label 'AIDS' must be understood as the arbitrary division of a spectrum, not as some absolute dividing line between health and ill-health or, implicitly, between life and a symbolic death. Also the enormous diversity of AIDS itself in terms of severity and specific manifestations must be outlined. The patient's own situation and prognosis should be located within such general outlines. It may be helpful to give examples of what has happened to similar patients in the past and what they were able to do after diagnosis. Such examples should be reasonably representative and credible; they may be particularly helpful if the patient knows or knows of particularly severe cases or clinical courses that may be (and often are) unrepresentative.

It is extremely important to state clearly during these discussions and, probably at this juncture, that one will be quite frank at all times, telling the patient everything one is thinking and expecting this to be mutual. This approach should also be apparent from one's manner before and after making such a statement. In particular, it should be emphasised that if one tells the patient that something is good news, one is not just jollying them along, but one really means it; on the other hand, if there is bad news to be told, then it will be told and the patient and clinician can face things together, taking appropriate action, mutually agreed.

Patients are typically relieved by this approach, even those whom others thought 'couldn't take it'. If after hearing bad news, patients wish to cope by exercising some form of denial, and this is a perfectly legitimate approach so long as the patient understands the real outlook at some level, then they are well able to exert selective memory of what has been said. This is another variation on the theme of patient choice. They can know what can be known and then remember what they wish. It is not for others, whether they be clinicians, lovers, family or anyone else, to decide what the patient should know. We usually underestimate people's ability to cope and have simplistic views about coping strategies. The way in which patients with AIDS have coped with their situation over the last few years after hearing all there is to hear about it, has shown that knowledge facilitates coping. Withholding it is dangerous and divisive and belongs to the world of paternalism.

On the specifics of the disease, the patient should understand that most of the infections in AIDS are not acquired from outside but are already latent within, so no purpose is generally served by isolating themselves from others. Exceptions, such as Salmonella, should be explained, with advice on how to avoid them by simple hygienic measures. On the other hand, patients should not go out of their way to catch ordinary infections, which is common sense. Certainly sexually transmitted infections and possibly other major infections can activate HIV, leading to further immune system damage.

The patient must understand the rationale and means of health maintenance in terms of the biology of AIDS and HIV. Good balanced nutrition as a way of avoiding cell-mediated immune defects resulting from dietary deficiency is an important part of the patient's role and can facilitate their personal involvement in care. Specific advice on how to achieve this may need involvement of a dietician. Patients should aim to put on weight, and to know that this is possible, not least to give them a little spare capacity in the event of intercurrent illness. Dietary advice of this sort, which must be flexible and take account of patient preferences, also helps to provide a basis of solid, biologically sound, advice against which the patient can assess the merits of the many 'alternative' diets they may be offered. The advantage of stopping smoking should be put in terms of how it will enhance pulmonary ciliary defence at a time when second line immune defence is impaired. Stopping smoking will also enhance appetite. Excessive alcohol should be avoided in view of its immunosuppressive effects.

While many lay advisers may put emphasis on avoiding stress, this can be confusing, misleading or frankly diversionary. Stress is all too vague a concept and I am unconvinced of its detrimental effects on the immune system. Some people are happiest when leading busy and active lives that others may perceive as stressful. To such a person the removal of this perceived stress may itself be stressful in another sense. People should be encouraged to go on being themselves. Making changes in their lives that are not 'them' seems just another way of letting the virus take control. Certainly, where patients can anticipate a good recovery from intercurrent events during AIDS, returning to work is an integral part of returning to normal life; it restores one of the normal threads of life that is essential to a person's integrity. Stopping work and sitting at home wondering what will happen next seems a most unsatisfactory approach to living well with

AIDS. On the other hand some patients, with the new perspective that the prognosis of AIDS necessitates, wish to do different things with the remainder of their lives. They should be helped in this, though any such decision should not be precipitate. Keeping fit generally seems sensible, but the approach must be compatible with the patient's own style.

Altogether the idea is to change and adapt those things that need to change, but not to feel the need to change everything, which may be unsettling, counterproductive and may be regretted later. Once patients appreciate the time-scale of their illness and the likelihood that they will remain well for some considerable time, they will find it easier not to turn everything upside down. A positive approach by the patient as a part of the team is underpinned and indeed effected by a personal involvement in, and commitment to, these aspects of the care programme. The health maintenance advice can be summarised as being all the things any good mother would tell you to do or not to do—common sense, boring perhaps, but wise.

The nature of the professional relationship should be defined and articulated and the patients must understand the logistics of the system. This must include ease of early access to skilled advice, should symptoms develop. This is not only reassuring to patients, in anticipation of such problems, but also ensures cost-effective management of intercurrent opportunist events, with shorter in-patient stays and greater emphasis on the patient staying well in the community. It is generally best to avoid giving the patient long lists of symptoms to look out for. These only encourage the adoption of the 'sick role' and foster body-checking, another rather negative approach. My usual advice is to say, listen to your body: you have lived with it for x years and you know how the 'usual' things, like ordinary coughs and colds feel; if you get anything out of the ordinary, get in touch and leave us to find out if it is important or not. Encouraging the patients to do this relieves anxiety, in advance and at the time, and ensures that the earlier symptoms are picked up.

The rationale and relative merits or otherwise of the various specific treatments, both for secondary events and for the underlying disease, must be discussed. This advice must be factual, well-informed and balanced. Consideration of the options, especially for newer or complementary treatments, should provide the patient with clear guidance through the miasma of conflicting claims (often exaggerated claims of benefit or equally exaggerated emphasis on toxicity). The decision regarding the choice must rest with the patient. Well-meaning advocacy by others may have given a patient a distorted view as to the likely benefit or otherwise of an experimental treatment in advance of good evidence. While the 'jungle telephone' is a very effective means of disseminating some information, the detail of the message can become dangerously distorted in its relaying. The rationale and design of clinical trials of new agents should be carefully explained, though the patient should feel no pressure to enter them. Some prefer to enter on the principle that they would like to do something, while others know their situation and may not want to 'rock the boat'. It is a matter of the patient's personal philosophy.

Patients must understand what type of illness they may get, not in terms of symptoms to look out for but so as to reassure that they are not, by and large, distressing, and that such symptoms can always be controlled while the underlying problem is dealt with. Some explanation of the nature, frequency and timing of HIV encephalopathy may be needed, as this is often a source of worry.

Issues concerning death and dying must be articulated at an early stage of discussion with the patient who has symptomatic disease. This is not to overemphasise this aspect, but rather to demystify it and also to place it explicitly on the agenda for future discussion when need be. Patients can only 'live with AIDS' effectively if they have resolved their conscious or unconscious fears about dying, how and where it will happen and what can be done in symptom control. This is especially important since so many of the messages all around them, such as those motivating others for behavioural change, inevitably emphasise the association between AIDS and death.

All these issues must be raised with the patient shortly after they have been given a diagnosis of AIDS (or ARC). This is a role for the senior clinician, who must be prepared to invest a great deal of time to this initial discussion. Indeed time must be set aside so that the patient feels the discussions are unhurried and open-ended and such a perception is reinforced by the demeanour and posture of the clinician. If this 'talk' is effectively done, it will set the scene for future discussions with the whole team, where the messages can be reiterated and spelt out in more detail as appropriate. The initial discussion will also ensure that patients' uncertainties, known and unknown, can be resolved pre-emptively. It can avert or reduce the risk that patients will keep 'bouncing back' because of unresolved fears or misunderstandings. In my view, this approach is not only optimal clinical management but is also cost-effective, by ensuring that patients understand their disease and the strategy for care in a way that utilises resources most efficiently.

The National Health Service, with its equitable principle of a tax-funded system of health care that is free at the point of delivery, has been a major asset in the management of people affected by costly chronic diseases, and AIDS has exemplified this very well. It has meant that the evolution of a clinically desirable but cost-effective model of care has been achievable without letting financial constraints impinge on the quality of care. That is not to say that clinicians have been unwilling or unable to confront the issues of cost and resources, rather that they have been able to argue the case for funding in the appropriate, i.e. political, arena without holding to ransom the individuals who were actually facing the problems of AIDS.

Another structural advantage in the UK was the network of sexually transmitted disease (STD) clinics set up as an alternative and open access primary care system. Many patients prefer not to discuss such problems with their family doctor. STD clinics had legally enforced protection of confidentiality that proved a great asset in the HIV epidemic. In addition, a number of such clinics had developed a reputation for being sympathetic to the needs of gay men, who bore the brunt of the initial epidemic in the UK. Indeed, it was this factor, together with the tendency of gay men to gravitate to parts of West London, that led to the emergence of the early centres of AIDS care. The STD clinics provided ideal locations for confidential counselling and, where appropriate, HIV testing when this became available. Their role in health education at a 'one-to-one' level, adjusting the messages to the specific dynamics of the person's actual situation remains a vital resource in prevention.

The system of primary care in the UK, with a central role for the general practitioner, represents a major resource for the coordination of care of patients between community and hospital sectors. While this important structural resource was initially under-utilised for a variety of reasons, the evolving strategies for care are increasingly and appropriately returning to the shared care model used for other serious chronic diseases. This is being achieved by defining, in respect of AIDS and HIV, the relative roles of hospital and general practitioner, the statutory roles of health and local authorities and the voluntary sector.

We also had the benefit in the UK of being able to witness the emerging problem of AIDS in the USA, which enabled some to recognise that the epidemic there and its consequences were the closest thing to a prophesy of what was to hit us a few years later. Of course, this advantage was constantly threatened by the denial phenomenon in some quarters. Nevertheless, clinicians in particular were able to develop links with the major US centres, to arrange training visits and a continuing dialogue on the development of care strategies. In hospitals this meant the creation of multidisciplinary care teams, though clinical responsibility remained under a single lead physician.

In the overall hospital or community service, some of the earliest issues to resolve concern infection control. These may have become confused by a variety of influences, including media coverage and pre-existing attitudes. Every centre will have to resolve these problems at an early stage to get over the 'hump', before effective systems of care can be implemented. Again the crucial element is openness, with frank discussion by leading clinicians and infection control staff with groups within the wider service about the nature of HIV, the evidence concerning its spread, the principles and practice of infection control, the importance of confidentiality and above all the ways in which different parts of the service are critical to the delivery of care to the patient. A sense of involvement in patient care by staff and an explicit understanding of their concerns by the front-line team can do much to defuse and resolve potential problems.

Another issue that comes up repeatedly is the one of centralisation, whether at hospital or ward level. In the emerging epidemic, there were strong arguments in favour of early centralisation of experience, where suitable care models could be developed and wide clinical experience gained. However, within a few years the emphasis has increasingly shifted towards transplanting the models established in these few centres to other hospitals both within London and elsewhere. While the early centres have continued to have a major concentration of patients, these increasingly derive from their local populations. They now have an important additional role in training staff from other centres, so that optimal care can be provided closer to the patient's home. The transition from tertiary referral to locally based specialist care is inevitably a gradual one and undue haste is potentially hazardous for individual patients. Fortunately, the activities of professional organisations, the Department of Health and Regional Health Authorities have helped to smooth the transition to a more appropriate balance of care between affected health districts.

Similarly, early clinical care within hospitals benefited from the centralisation of experience in designated wards, such as infectious diseases wards. This served to concentrate experience for the establishment of care models and to ensure adequate staff training. These could then go on to train others within the hospital and elsewhere as AIDS/HIV-related issues increasingly presented elsewhere. There remain strong arguments for some degree of centralisation since the complex clinical and social issues that arise require considerable special skills and familiarity. Nevertheless, other wards and staff must become attuned to these issues sufficiently to be able to deal with the problems that will increasingly fall within their remit. In addition, there is much to be said for having something of a case-mix on the designated wards so that while they deal predominantly with AIDS/HIV, other patient groups are seen. This helps to preserve confidentiality, maintain staff morale and ensure a balanced training programme for ward staff.

Although initial expertise in AIDS inevitably developed in hospitals, many centres are now actively seeking to redress the balance of care to incorporate community-based agencies and general practitioners. The most effective of means for achieving this at our centre has been the setting up of a hospital-based Home Support Team of nursing staff and a specially trained GP. The team has helped individual patients through the transition to home after acute admission and draw in and/or provide community-based care in the patient's home as necessary. In drawing in the statutory and voluntary agencies, they can help to train staff in these agencies and help them over their own 'humps'. Most importantly they can help to identify the relative roles of the different agencies in a shared care model. This has proved very effective, with increasing proportions of patients receiving care from community-based agencies rather than from the team itself, while the team increasingly adopts a training and facilitating role. Ideally such a team should render itself obsolete, so long as all the elements of care are taken in hand by relevant agencies.

41

Fortunately, some of the early lacunae in local authority services are being remedied and some authorities have taken an excellent lead. For patients in need of residential facilities during convalescence, for respite care and terminal care, centres have evolved, such as the London Lighthouse and Mildmay Mission, which cater specifically for people with AIDS. They complement the important involvement of some existing hospices, which have widened their horizons to take on patients with AIDS in a mixed setting, which may suit some patients better.

Voluntary sector involvement has been a major part of community-based care in London, though not to the extent that it has in San Francisco. Buddy schemes are well established, for example that provided by the Terrence Higgins Trust, which also provides legal and welfare rights advice, not to mention excellent information and helpline programmes for information and prevention. The Lighthouse has its own home support team, volunteer training and counselling groups. One of the most important developments has been the creation of groups of people with HIV infection (Body Positive) and with AIDS (Frontliners), whose work in self-help, advice and advocacy has been especially thoughtful and compelling because of their unique perspective. The booklet 'Living with AIDS', produced by Frontliners, is a superb resource of information which we give to every newly diagnosed patient. It provides them with an excellent factual base and a continuing sense of community with others in the same situation.

We must continue to improve our caring response by listening to and learning from our patients and learning from our mistakes. The positive approach and extraordinary personal resourcefulness of our patients are a source of strength and motivation in this difficult task. The continuous process of learning will help us to widen our perspectives and to enhance our effectiveness in responding to the aspirations of our patients and the demands of this terrible epidemic. We can also translate and adapt the models of care that have developed for AIDS to the treatment of a wide range of other clinical problems.

DISCUSSION

Audience Dr Pinching, you have dealt for so long with your AIDS patients, a lot of powerful emotions must have been released. How have you coped with these personal feelings over the years?

Dr Pinching A lot of people have asked me that and it may seem very facile to say, but I cope only because of the way the patients cope. I find that people respond positively to help to a degree that I could never imagine myself doing, and I find their fortitude keeps me going. If you are still learning from your patients, learning about how people do cope, then actually it helps you cope yourself. However, anyone working in this or similar fields must ensure that they have access to counselling support themselves. Often this is best arranged off-site with a counsellor not on the care team itself.

Dr Hull It is a strange point to make, but perhaps AIDS is a blessing in disguise in that it is drawing us back to a much older method of delivering care, one which we have sadly lacked in this century, and that is one of listening to and serving our patients.

Audience Dr Pinching, at the moment you probably see a large proportion of the people with AIDS in this country. What provision is being made to train others to do the same counselling throughout the country?

Dr Pinching Here we are, this is a start. One of the problems of training people in this particular aspect is that good counselling has got to be done on a one-to-one basis, without an audience. You can train partly by the attitude you employ and the specifics you mention; you can train to some extent by writing about it or speaking about it. Several courses are now being run locally and nationally and there are also a number of books available on the subject. Videos may be helpful, although you cannot record the real situation because the counselling process itself could be affected by video recording; using a good actor in a simulation would be a possibility. It is absolutely crucial that some training does occur, by whatever means. However, some things can only be learnt by direct involvement. I am not a formally trained counsellor and yet I have been trained by experience.

FOREWORD: AFTERNOON SESSION

The afternoon was devoted to exploring how communication, particularly about bad news, might be taught. Dr Robin Hull demonstrated a teaching method used with medical students at Birmingham and Dr Brian McAvoy stressed that communication skills can be learned, that they are an integral part of good practice and that an effective method of teaching is by means of simulated patients and video-recording.

This session was more audience participative than the morning and led to some brisk exchanges of views. There was strong criticism of medical education as being scientific and reductionist echoing the views of Kerr White in his important report of the Dialogue at Wickenburg.[1] There is insufficient emphasis on communication skills, which in some cases seem to worsen during medical training. Though this was defended by some specialists there was a general feeling that medicine needed a human face, an awareness of the emotional needs of people facing news of mutilation, severe illness or death. Imparting this information poses enormous stress to doctors who, inadequately prepared for it, sometimes renege on their communication responsibilities. In consequence they offer a poor example to students. The teaching of communication skills is fundamental to medical education and requires a prominent place in the mainstream of the medical curriculum. If this does not occur then medicine would be better to recognise that other professional groups are often better communicators than doctors.

This poses the question: should doctors leave it to them or learn to do it better?

DR R HULL
Macmillan Senior Lecturer in General Practice
University of Birmingham

REFERENCE

1 White K L. The Task of Medicine; Dialogue at Wickenburg. The Henry J. Kaiser Family Foundation. Menlo Park, California. 1988.

THE BREAST LUMP
IN GENERAL PRACTICE

Dr R Hull
Macmillan Senior Lecturer in General Practice
University of Birmingham

This chapter records the discussion that was generated by considering the case of a 35 year old woman who presented to her general practitioner with a breast lump. The situation had been acted professionally, video-recorded, and was played to the conference audience.

To assist in this participative session a discussion panel sat in front of the audience and consisted:

(1) Professor Michael Baum,
     Professor of Surgery,
     King's College Hospital, London
(2) Annalee Curran, General Practice Counsellor,
     Department of General Practice,
     King's College School of Medicine and Dentistry, London
(3) Lesley Fallowfield, Lecturer in Health Psychology,
     Academic Unit of Psychiatry,
     London Medical School
(4) Dr Roger Higgs,
     Director and Senior Lecturer,
     Department of General Practice,
     King's College School of Medicine and Dentistry, London

Each scene raises many questions and shows how our attempts to communicate as health professionals, with our patients and each other, may be made more difficult, may be misguided, or simply inappropriate. The responses by the panel and audience do not aim to be comprehensive, rather they are a collection of views of caring individuals documented and given in the hope that they may induce further debate, and ultimately cause progress in this difficult area.

I would like to start with a quotation from Albert Schweitzer:

It is our duty to remember at all times and anew that medicine is not only a science, but also the art of letting our own individuality interact with the individuality of the patient. [Quoted in Strauss M B. *Familiar Medical Quotations*. Little, Brown and Company. Boston. 1968]

Sequence 1

SOUND	VISION
	Roger and Mary Snow call at their doctor's busy surgery. They seem hesitant, he protective, she obviously anxious. He sits her down and approaches the receptionist who is very young and
Roger: Hello, we haven't got an appointment but is it possible to see Dr. Phillips today? My wife's a bit upset, she found a lump last night when she was showering.	inexperienced. There is another receptionist training her. At the mention of a lump the older receptionist nods and they all turn to look at Mary.

Prof Baum The situation is clearly exaggerated, but it points out the profound influence upon patients of the paramedical staff who have contact with them. We often forget this.

Dr Higgs The scene reminded me of some of the problems that receptionists face. To judge from the comments given at a recent receptionist course, many of them feel 'in the middle'. I do not think we prepare them for this: they are actually working for two completely different sets of people. They are employed by the practice and the doctor, but they are also working for the patients, a relationship which imposes a different set of rules and problems. In fact it was clear that some of the receptionists felt sometimes that there was information which they should withhold from the doctors because they felt that the doctors could not cope with it. This is a truth-telling issue which we should consider exploring.

Dr Hull Patients often want to talk at their own level, and if this is blocked, we have created a barrier.

Audience Her fear will create a barrier which we must acknowledge.

Dr Fallowfield It is not typical for women to take their husbands along with them at this stage. Many women are very frightened when they find a breast lump and do not disclose it to their husbands.

Audience The lack of privacy at the point of contact with the receptionist is a barrier.

Dr Hull Yes, but if you visit general practices throughout the land you will find reception areas boxed-off, which will cause difficulties later on.
   Will the perceived diagnosis create a barrier?

Prof Baum A recent audit of referrals from general practitioners to my

46

breast clinic over a two-year period, of women like this who find a lump, showed that half have nothing wrong, and of those that do have a lump, the chances of it being a cancer at her age are about 1 in 20. Nevertheless, she will still be very anxious.

Dr Hull I suggest the lesion is problem number 2; the main concern is anxiety, because her fear is cancer. That is the problem that has to be dealt with initially. The trouble is we tend to be terribly sympathetic to the people who have cancer, but have less time, less kindness, for the people who merely think that they have cancer.

Sequence 2

Time: Follows on from sequence 1   Consulting room. Dr writing
Knock   Roger and Mary enter
Dr: Come in.   Dr gets up to meet them
I haven't seen you two for a long   Shakes hands, Roger first
time.
Mary: No, thank goodness we've
all been very well.   Roger and Mary sit at corner of
                                     desk, close together, holding
Dr: Good. So what brings you to   hands
see me?
Roger: Well, it's Mary. She asked
me to come. She has found this
lump. . .   Fade

Dr Higgs It is important to establish first contact with the patient. The greeting of the husband first, and the way in which the contact was established concerns me.

Audience The woman was displaying sickness signals, which the doctor had not perceived.

Dr Hull The anxiety of a patient has been built up. Did you, notice in the first scene, how when the husband said, 'She's got a breast lump,' everybody turned and looked at her. She was immediately someone apart from the crowd, being separated from everyone else, she was a sick woman.

GP Trainee I liked the way he greeted them at the door and sat them down, at least he was not buried in papers and notes.

Audience The first point is that the doctor should have addressed the couple by their names and not shaken hands only with the man and not the woman.

47

Should he not go out into the waiting room and invite them into his room?

Dr Hull I agree, these additions would change the whole dynamics of the situation for the better. I was advocating this behaviour recently with a group of GPs in Cheltenham. The older GPs were absolutely incensed at the waste of time this would cause. The younger GPs had introduced it and discovered that there were tremendous advantages: you can see what is happening in the waiting room, and you can see that there is somebody ill in the corner and that they ought to be seen soon. You can watch the patient walk down the corridor and see the way she moves. A whole host of non-verbal communication is passed.

Sequence 3

Time: Follows from sequence 2	Consulting room. Dr, Mary and Roger
Dr: A lump in your breast?	Dr leaning forward, concerned
Mary: Yes. I found it last night when I was showering and washing just here . . . It's not very big but . . .	She looks down at breast. . . . . . and touches right breast He leans further forward watching her intently
Dr: What do you think might cause it?	
Mary: Thats what we've come to see you about.	
Dr: Yes of course. What do you fear might cause it?	
Mary: I'm terrified it might be cancer, you see my mum died of cancer. She was only 35, just like me.	Roger and Mary exchange glances

Dr Hull At this stage, is it a good idea to be talking about cancer?

Prof Baum It is not a bad idea. I often say, 'You think you have got cancer, well, let's be open about it.'

Dr Hull But for some I see there are still reservations. People say, 'Let's wait until we have got the definitive answer, and the path. report back.' Some of my students say, 'Let's wait till we have examined her.' But when you are examining somebody with a hard, craggy lump in the breast, they know from your face what is going on. Unless you bring the question out early, one is leaving the patient to interpret the non-verbal signals, which may make things worse.

Sequence 4

Time: Follows from sequence 3

Dr: You know most breast lumps in a lady of your age are quite benign. Listen, I would like to ask you a lot of questions, then I shall examine you. After that I might be able to tell you. . . If I do think it's cancer . . . do you want me to tell you?
pause
Mary: Yes . . . I've got to know.
Dr: Roger?
Roger: . . . Yes . . . I Suppose so.

Consulting room. Dr, Mary and Roger
Dr watching Mary
Dr rubbing his ear

Mary drops her eyes at question, twisting her hands

Roger glances at Doctor, then as he speaks, looks at Mary. Fade

Dr Higgs I want to acknowledge the two diagnoses, cancer and the fear. It is very important to give these equal status in our decision making and our discussion. I should want to make it clear that I had heard her worry about cancer, but I had also heard her worry. Unless I can convince her that I am that sort of doctor which hears both, I would feel I was beginning to fail.

Dr Hull What is going through the mind of the young husband, whose wife has found a lump in her breast?

Mrs Curran Fear of cancer and of losing her.

Dr Higgs 'I am frightened about the process of being a patient, of being under a doctor's control.' We assume that patients do not feel this when they come to us, otherwise, we reason, they would not attend. If I think about myself facing an operation, I begin to feel I do not like the people I am meeting when I am talking about that awful eventuality.

Dr Hull We see then the development of a relationship between a man and his wife, a difficult relationship between both of them and their doctor, and overall an intense amount of fear.

Sequence 5

Time: A few minutes later

Consulting room. Roger alone looking out of window, hands in pockets waiting. Mary enters adjusting dress. Dr follows shutting door. Mary does not meet Roger's eye. Dr reassuringly gestures them to sit. They do so, again holding hands.

Dr: Well, I've had a good look at Mary and I'm very pleased to tell you that it has all the characteristics of a benign lump. Nevertheless I do feel that you ought to see a surgeon.

Dr leans forward looking closely at them.
R and M turn to each other smiling at the word benign.

Mary: That means losing a breast.

Dr taken aback

Dr: Wait a minute, you're crossing too many bridges. . . What we should do is to remove the lump and look at it under the microscope. No decision will be made until then . . . but I can tell you I feel pretty certain that it's benign. . . .

M turns to R, sighs and rests her head on his shoulder . . . Pause. . . R glances doubtfully at Dr. Fade

Audience You should not use medical language. She did not understand what 'benign' means.

Dr Hull Exactly, so often we talk down to patients and use words that they may not understand, which leads to distancing.

Audience The doctor has given her the false impression that there is a high chance that he will be able to know if it is benign or malignant.

As a result the trust of the husband is lost, because he is quite sure that the doctor is not telling the truth, having decided to send his wife to a surgeon. It would have been helpful to have tackled that dilemma at the beginning.

Prof Baum The GP has been in too much of a hurry to offer reassurance and missed an important clue in the history. Her family history is bad enough, but when the mother had breast cancer at a very early age, then she has an exceedingly high risk. Immediately the risk of breast cancer changes from 1:20 to 1:2. Secondly, the diagnostic processes described were probably inaccurate. The GP must know which clinician he is working with at the hospital and his diagnostic and therapeutic preferences.

Dr Hull The lesson appears to be, 'Don't put oneself in a position from which one has to back down.'

Sequence 6

Time: Some weeks later just before Christmas

Dr: Ah here we are
How did you get on at the hospital?
M: They didn't tell me very much.
Dr: You know what it's like, they're so busy. The surgeon wrote to me, he agreed with my findings and that it should come out to be 100% sure. P'raps you'd like to see the letter?. . .
. . . O.K. come and see me after the operation so I can see how you are. . . Bye

Consulting room. Dr and Mary Dr examining records with M sitting beside him. He finds hospital letter and turns to her.

She smiles, nodding

He gives her the letter
She takes it and smiles as she reads it.
Dr generally reassuring and dismissive

Prof Baum Delays are intolerable, not because it is a surgical emergency, which it is not, but because it is a psychological emergency. I feel that such delays actually occur infrequently.

I do not see the point of that interview at all. It is totally useless and a waste of the woman's time. This is not a criticism of the general practitioner but of the surgeon at the hospital. I recommend strongly that patients with a breast lump are referred to a specialist who will carry out the investigations promptly, who will counsel the woman accurately and organise the patient's admission immediately.

Dr Hull Who wants to respond? I don't think we all agree.

Audience Most patients are going to be too frightened in many situations to share their fears with a doctor or surgeon whom they have met only once. They will be grateful for the opportunity to talk to their family doctor, a familiar face whom they have met many times before, and trust.

Dr Hull I believe that to be absolutely essential and totally disagree with you, Professor Baum. It is very important for the patient to come back to the old, known friend. She can make contact with him and say, 'What did the surgeon mean when he said so and so? To be quite honest I was a bit frightened and I did not quite hear all he said.'

51

Prof Baum That is because the counselling service offered in the hospital is misunderstood. It is *not* anonymous, and the whole purpose is to recognise the problems of communication and to employ professionals to handle the difficulty promptly, so that the patients do understand and have ample opportunity to discuss their fears.

The video is also perpetuating the myth that all surgeons are hopeless at communicating and that is incorrect. One of the great pleasures for most surgeons is to be able to say with confidence to a woman, 'It is not cancer. You are OK.' It is immensely satisfying.

Dr Higgs I feel it is important for the GP to promise the opportunity to go through it all with the patient, but I also agree with Professor Baum that this consultation demonstrated a missed opportunity. So many very important issues still exist and could have been discussed, in spite of the negative findings: the one in two risk of cancer due to the family history, what she has to say about her mother dying at the age of 35; whether that has been faced completely, whether it has completely ruined her life, whether it has made a difference to her relationship with her husband or whether she has never forgiven her mother. This could be *the* diagnosis. So, unfortunately, because we failed to keep the two diagnoses in our mind, the fear and the cancer, the cancer only has been pursued and the fear associated with cancer has not.

Dr Hull Many GPs would agree with that, but would say that the problem of time is ever present.

Audience I feel strongly that it is not the GP's role to delve deeply into problems which she may not want to discuss, for example, her relationship with her mother.

Dr Hull She was not given a chance.

Audience She gave no clue, visual or verbal.

Dr Hull Well, what possible clues did you pick up there to suggest that she did *not* want to speak about other problems?

Audience She seemed happy.

Dr Hull English people keep a stiff upper lip. She is doing that.

Audience Does she need to be reduced to tears? What is wrong with a stiff upper lip? It does not mean we are less caring professionals.

Dr Hull There is always this room for debate. I do feel that when we as general practitioners refer a patient to an expert, we think, 'Good, she is now in safe hands.' We must not forget that the patient actually needs continued care and support from the general practitioner as well. We must not lose track of the woman, because if we do and it becomes a malignant condition requiring palliative and later terminal care at home, we will have lost trust and so justifying the look seen in her husband's eyes at the end of that video sequence.

Audience What does the panel think of you letting the patient see the letter without the permission of the consultant? What will you do if she develops cancer later on? Would you show her the letter?

Panel Unanimously, yes.

Prof Baum My patients often sit in as I am dictating. I quite like them to hear what is to be written. There are occasional opportunities when private communication between the consultant and the GP is needed. The questioner has picked out however that you are now on a hook, thereafter she will expect you to show every letter.

Mrs Curran I feel that the handling of that letter was a most empty gesture. He said, 'Here you can see that we are not saying one thing and meaning another,' but of course he is thinking something else. That is the other agenda, it may not be benign and this is not being addressed.

Sequence 7

Time: Early in New Year	CAPTION The biopsy report shows an anaplastic carcinoma

Dr Higgs As the general practitioner I would know we would have to have a frank discussion about what it means to her. I would find it very difficult. One of the major problems is that we do not acknowledge how difficult it is to do this. That is why we do not do it very well, because we do not practise it properly.

Dr Hull We have not talked about this, the doctor is frightened, and he hates doing it.

Audience I should be petrified to have a conversation with this woman; she has been told far too many times that everything is all right. When are you going to give her the opportunity to be listened to and how? The GP must face this problem with her, and address the fact that she does not trust the information because of previously false reassurances. The GP must decide whether to call her to his surgery or visit at home.

Prof Baum There is a great flaw in the whole scenario. There is an implied assumption that the surgeon is only the technician, and that the GP is doing all the communicating. It is not like that these days. Left to the surgeon the whole thing should have been over in August. The diagnosis would have been known before she had the biopsy using modern technology. The GP is supplementing the counselling and information that she has been given at the hospital.

Dr Hull Sadly, GPs still say that they have had to break the news of malignancy to patients on occasion.

Sequence 8

Time: Later that day
Doorbell

Mary: Come through into the kitchen Dr. I'll make some coffee. I'm just in the middle of making cakes. Look at me . . . covered in flour.

Mary's home. M is seen in kitchen using mixer with flour on hands. She runs to front door
Dr seen struggling out of wet rain-coat wiping rain off specs. He follows her slowly into kitchen and leans on wall.

Dr: Mary, is Roger at home?
M: No, I don't expect him for ages. Is anything wrong?
Dr: I've just had a phone call from the hospital. . . .

She closes her eyes, and freezes, then looks down at her hands, shaking her head, then looks him straight in the eye.

M: You don't need to tell me, I can see it in your face.
Dr: We all thought it was benign. . . but but I'm afraid it is malignant. . . .

Her face puckers but she rallies and looks him straight in the face

Mrs Fallowfield It is wrong to break bad news out of the blue. You should not call on the woman in the middle of cooking and say, 'Hey, guess what?' You must ensure that the patient is going to have somebody around to help them once you have delivered the bad news. Invite her to come along to the surgery with her mum, her best friend or her dad with her; it is terribly important.

Prof Baum This approach leaves the patient very vulnerable. I came with the prejudice that bad news is bad news and it does not matter how you break it, but having seen that, I now realise there are bad ways to break bad news.

Mrs Curran I am worried about the term '*breaking* bad news.' Breaking is exactly what has happened, she is shattered. It is interesting that she said, 'I knew it.' 'News' is not always news. Perhaps examining the phrase 'breaking bad news' would give us some clues about how we could do it better, rather than dropping this bombshell.

Prof Baum There is plenty of evidence from our own work with breast cancer patients that the presence by invitation and consent of the patient of her primary source of support at the bad news consultation significantly improves the outcome a year later, as measured by anxiety and depression scores, and adjustment.

Dr Higgs I am disorientated by the fact that this is such an alien method. I find it hard to get inside. It has been set up as a diverging pathway between two people who ought to be working together. It seems often that we set up confrontational situations with our patients, instead of saying, 'Let's look at this problem side by side', and creating a situation where the issue can be shared.

Dr Hull As a member of the audience said earlier it was right at the beginning, in the first consultation, that the mistake was made, and if it hadn't been it would be easier now.

Audience What has been said underlines many of the differences between general practice, where people attend often, and hospitals, where people come along at set intervals for their appointment, every month or two months. It is therefore only in general practice that the question of visiting/phoning/inviting to the surgery will arise.

Prof Baum Can I re-emphasise that I do not believe that the GP should be giving the diagnosis at all. There is an old saying that compassion without knowledge is fraudulent, and however compassionate a doctor he might be, it is essential that he has the full knowledge of what happens next when he gives the diagnosis. As a GP he will not know what is going to happen next, because of the rapid development in this area. This knowledge is only immediately available to the consultant, who should be giving the diagnosis.

Audience Although the topic under discussion is breast cancer, there are lots of other diagnoses that GPs have to give that do not fall into this category of going to a specialist and returning for support. We must not forget the generality by homing in on the specific. There are a whole range of topics and issues requiring good communication, in which the GP has an important complementary role. I tend to disagree with the point that the patient will be unsupported following a visit by the GP. If a patient has had a cot-death you do not invite the patient to come to the surgery with a relative. In General Practice there is a whole team providing support to that patient and you will not simply give the diagnosis to the patient and then forget her. You are going to continue the conversation as to what is going to happen next, 'who is at home, when will your husband be back and who are you going to discuss it with?' The Health Visitor and social workers will also be involved.

Remaining Scenes

Mary does very well following her encounter with the surgeon and 18 months goes by before she reappears in the doctor's surgery having hurt her back working in the garden. X-rays show metastases in her lumbar spine. Radiotherapy and chemotherapy follow. She says to the District Nurse when visiting that the cure is worse than the disease and there is difficulty in knowing whether to continue. She responds well; but after another 6 months she develops a malignant pleural effusion, rapidly goes into terminal care and is dying at home. The husband by this time is overstressed, becomes alcoholic and cannot cope at work. Events pile up and eventually the lady is admitted to a hospice where she dies. Finally the video deals with the bereavement of the husband.

Dr Hull The afternoon produced much healthy disagreement, which was marvellous. As soon as people start disagreeing they can challenge themselves about the way to communicate.

Finally, if we are to communicate with our patient, we must be able to communicate with ourselves.

POSTSCRIPT

A printed presentation of a long but brisk interaction between a large audience in an auditorium and a panel of experts conveys little feel of the atmosphere of controversy and dispute. Everyone in the room was thinking: they had to because any one of them might be asked to comment at any time.

The important lesson to emerge was that there is no one right way of breaking bad news; which, as Schweitzer pointed out, depends on the unique combination of the individuals concerned. The best preparation for this task, which unhappily falls to us all as both givers and receivers of bad news, is by being sensitive to the variety of means of communication. Such sensitivity is enhanced by exercises such as this.

The videotape 'Telling the Truth' and its accompanying tutor's instructions is available from Dr Robin Hull, Macmillan Senior Lecturer in Palliative Care, Department of General Practice, the Medical School, Birmingham University, Birmingham B15 2TJ.

HANDLING COMMUNICATION PROBLEMS IN GENERAL PRACTICE

Brian R McAvoy
Senior Lecturer
Department of General Practice, University of Leicester

INTRODUCTION

Can communication skills be taught and learned, and, if so, how? When considering communication in medicine it is important to:

(i) Describe the importance and relevance of communication skills;
(ii) Highlight the evidence for the lack and inadequate teaching of these abilities;
(iii) Outline alternative methods of teaching and learning.

Breaking bad news is a particularly powerful illustration of the need for good communication skills. It is also necessary to look at the broader importance and relevance of such techniques.

IMPORTANCE AND RELEVANCE OF COMMUNICATION SKILLS

The General Medical Council's Recommendations on Basic Medical Education state 20 objectives, two of which relate specifically to communication skills:

To be able to communicate effectively and sensitively with (a) patients and their relatives, and (b) with medical colleagues and other health professionals.

There is now considerable evidence to suggest that the ability to communicate has a major influence on the:

(i) adequacy of the consultation;
(ii) patients' satisfaction;
(iii) patients' compliance;
(iv) patients' response to investigation and treatment;
(v) doctors' relationships with their colleagues.

(i) Adequacy of Consultation

Sir James Spence described the consultation as the essential unit of medical practice. It has two parts: The interview in which the doctor tries to ascertain why the patient has consulted, and the exposition in which he explains his conclusions and advises the patient. Success in both parts depends largely on communication skills.

The key to success in the interview is good history-taking. Hampton and colleagues have shown that in over 80% of medical out-patients the final diagnosis and management was predicted on the basis of the history alone; physical examination and laboratory investigations played a relatively minor role.[1] Sandler confirmed that the history was the most important element in medical out-patient consultations, deciding 56% of all diagnoses and 46% of subsequent management schemes.[2]

'Good history taking' involves far more than administering a long list of questions; in the words of Michael Balint, 'If the doctor asks questions in the manner of medical history-taking, he will always get answers—but hardly anything more.' The doctor needs to listen carefully, noting not only *what* the patient is saying but also *how* it is being said (the paralinguistics). Moreover he must be aware of, and able to interpret, the wealth of non-verbal communication present in the consultation.

(ii) Patients' Satisfaction

Surveys in general practice and hospital in both Great Britain and the United States have consistently shown that a considerable number of patients are dissatisfied with the medical care they have received.[3] The commonest source of this dissatisfaction is poor communication; recorded in as many as 51% of patients attending general practice and 65% in hospital. Patients' satisfaction with consultations has been found to correlate well with three aspects of doctors' behaviour; meeting patients' expectations, dealing with their worries and concerns, and perceived friendliness. The same study found no correlation between satisfaction and the diagnosis, length of consultation, waiting time, or the social class or educational status of the patients. Patients seem to be dissatisfied with *what is* and *is not said* to them, rather than with *what is done* medically.

(iii) Patients' Compliance

Non-compliance with medical advice is common. Reviewing 68 studies of patients' compliance in following advice on medicine taking, diet, exercise, etc., Ley found a non-compliance rate of nearly 50%.[4] Such behaviour can render treatment ineffective, result in hospital admissions and waste money. Compliance with advice correlated well with the patients' satisfaction with the consultation, with the communication that took place, and the medical care received. Putting it simply, satisfied patients are more likely to comply.

Patients' non-compliance can be explained in terms of two factors:

(i)   failure to *understand* what is said;
(ii) failure to *remember* what is said.

Understanding, recall and ultimate compliance can be improved by employing specific techniques:

(i)   providing the more important information first;
(ii)   stressing the importance of the information;
(iii)   using simple language;
(iv)   presenting the material in separate categories;
(v)   repeating information;
(vi)   making advice specific, detailed and concrete.

These skills can be learned and improved.

(iv)   Patients' Response to Investigation and Treatment

Providing information and support to patients before investigations or operations is beneficial. Patients undergoing endoscopy were studied: The group who received an explanation of the likely sensations they would experience required fewer tranquillisers and were less restless during the procedure.

(v)   Doctors' Relationships with their Colleagues

Communication skills are an essential part of everyday practice, whether in hospital or the community. GPs, hospital doctors and other health care professionals communicate on a daily basis by letter and telephone. Good communication helps patients' care, and enhances job satisfaction.

EVIDENCE FOR LACK OF COMMUNICATION SKILLS
AND INADEQUATE TEACHING

Poor communication has been shown to be the commonest cause of patient dissatisfaction with medical care. Junior hospital doctors may use a style of interviewing which bombards patients with direct questions and discourages them from disclosing emotional problems. Patients' questions are often ignored and enquiry about mood, reaction to illness or the effect on the family avoided.

Experienced hospital doctors have been found to respond rarely to verbal and non-verbal cues given by patients about their emotional state. In a study with breast cancer patients, despite evidence of the patients being distressed, surgeons enquired directly about the possibility of emotional problems in only 5% of cases.[5] Another study involved paediatricians with up to five years' experience and demonstrated that while most thought that they had been friendly during the interviews, less than half of the patients agreed.[6]

Similar results are seen in general practice. Family doctors in training fail to detect and record a substantial proportion of problems even when revealed spontaneously by their patients.[7] Irrespective of experience, general practitioners have been found to dominate consultations, seek to prevent or stifle expressions of feeling, make few empathic statements, fail to meet patients' eyes, avoid personal issues and minimise social and psychological factors. In a study designed to quantify the detection of psychiatric illness amongst patients, the practitioners' ability ranged from 20% to 80%. Success was *not* related to the amount of time spent with the patients but strongly correlated with the effective use of history-taking techniques.[8]

Maguire suggests that neglect in medical schools to teach such a vital area of clinical need is based on four assumptions:[9]

(i) doctors possess these skills;
(ii) doctors cannot acquire them;
(iii) using these skills will create problems;
(iv) these skills have no important effect on care.

The first and last assumptions have been tackled. The second is based on the belief that such skills are a gift of God—'You are either born with them or not.' Such a fatalistic attitude implies that deficiencies cannot be remedied. There is now considerable evidence that many of these skills *can* be taught. Admittedly, some individuals are better communicators than others, but as with all social skills, training and practice can lead to improvement. Medical students' performance in interviewing has been shown to improve after training sessions involving audio or video tape feedback. The improvement was greater than with traditional methods and the students preferred video to audiotape. They improved at eliciting accurate and relevant information, exerting more appropriate control over the interview and exploring personal but relevant issues such as marriage, sexual adjustment and the possibility of suicidal ideas. Their understanding of the patients' emotional feelings developed.

The assumption that using these skills will create problems are related to doctors' anxieties in dealing with certain groups of patients, for example, those who are angry, refuse to accept advice, have chronic illnesses or are dying. It is precisely these patients who so often require the bad news to be broken skilfully. By communicating effectively with such patients, doctors will open up sensitive and painful issues. This process can be stressful, and some avoid these issues by concentrating on the physical aspects of a complaint. Refusing to acknowledge the value of communication skills training may be part of a defence mechanism on the part of the doctor.

TEACHING AND LEARNING COMMUNICATION SKILLS

The end product of such teaching is a practical skill and the emphasis should be on learning by doing. Unsupervised experience is not particularly valuable. Observation and feedback are essential features of the techniques, and lead to improvement. Exploring and understanding attitudes (both patients' and doctors') are integral parts of learning about communication skills and small-group work can help. Many courses employ both individual and group work.

Teaching methods associated with passive learning include lectures and the use of didactic materials such as books, films and pre-recorded videotapes.

Active learning involves the following techniques:

1. Modified essay questions
2. Small group discussions
3. Role play
4. Direct observation
5. Review of audio or videotapes

At Leicester University General Practice is taught in all five years of the curriculum, but the principal contribution is a five-week full-time course in the 4th year. The students attend in groups of 20. The teaching programme involves 4 days per week of practice attachment and 1 day per week of departmental teaching. The methods used in the Department include:

- patient management questionnaires
- case discussions
- a group project
- mini-lectures
- small group exercises/workshops
- analysis of videorecorded consultations
- consultations with simulated patients

The latter is a valid, powerful and relevant teaching method: The simulated patients are authentic. If properly trained, they are indistinguishable from real patients, and this has been proved in several studies with experienced physicians. Their performances are consistent and reproducible, but adjustable so they can be adapted for undergraduate or postgraduate use. Simulated patients, unlike real patients, are readily available. Perhaps most importantly they are 'safe'. They can be used to try out various approaches to difficult and problematic situations—such as breaking bad news—without risk. If the student has difficulty or dries up, nobody gets hurt. Different strategies can be tried and their relative merits and demerits compared. The sessions can end with direct feedback from the 'patient'. This is a powerful element of the learning experience and one rarely encountered during a student's career.

Students get the opportunity to be videorecorded consulting with the simulated patients. They receive feedback on their performance in a one-to-one teaching session with the GP tutor. Non-verbal skills ('body language') are also studied and improved.

Simulated patients can be used also in the teaching and evaluation of problem solving and management skills.

SUMMARY

1. Communication skills are an integral part of good clinical practice—they are *not* an optional extra or icing on the cake.
2. They have a major influence on the consultation and enhance patients' satisfaction and compliance.
3. Communication skills *can* be learned and improved. Training *is* effective and feasible: One of the most effective methods is to use simulated patients and videorecording.

REFERENCES

1 Hampton J R, Harrison M J G, Mitchell J R A *et al.* Relative contributions of history-taking, physical examination, and laboratory investigation to diagnosis and management of medical outpatients. *Br Med J* 1975;2:486–9.

2 Sandler G. Costs of unnecessary tests. *Br Med J* 1979;2:21–4.

3 Ley P. Patients' understanding and recall in clinical communication failure. In: Pendleton D and Hasler J. eds *Doctor-Patient Communication.* London: Academic Press, 1983, pp 89–107.

4 Ley P. Satisfaction, compliance and communication. *Br J Clin Psychol* 1982;21:241–54.

5 Maguire P. The psychological and social sequelae of mastectomy. In: Howells J G. ed. *Modern Perspectives in the Psychiatric Aspects of Surgery.* New York: Bruner Mazel. 1976:390–421.

6 Korsch B M, Negrette V F. Doctor-patient communication. Scientific American 1972;227:66–73.

7 Bentsen B G. The accuracy of recording patient problems in family practice. Journal of Medical Education 1976;51:331–16.

8 Marks J N, Goldberg D P, Hillier V F. Determinants of the ability of general practitioners to detect psychiatric illness. Psychological Medicine 1979;9:337–53.

9 Maguire P. Doctor-patient skills. In: Social Skills and Health. Ed Argyll M. London: Methuen, 1981:56–81.

DISCUSSION

Audience   Do you have medical students who find this communication skills ability so hard to master that they consider giving up, and if so, how do you deal with it?

Dr McAvoy   Some do discuss their anxieties in dealing with this type of teaching, but they appreciate that this is a helpful method of trying to deal with these same concerns, rather than being 'dropped in it' on the wards, once qualified. There might be a danger in introducing this method at too early a stage. As you have seen, it is a stressful experience and the tutor does have to de-role the students at the end of the afternoon. Our teaching takes place in the fourth year and they will have had between one and two years of clinical practice by this time, and I am sure this avoids problems. One student had been thinking seriously about giving up medicine before she started these sessions, but found that the experience of one to one close involvement with patients confirmed her desire to continue.

Audience Dr McAvoy, speaking as a medical student, is not the training you are giving simply a form of remedial therapy? Should not our consultants be teaching and displaying these skills throughout our medical school education? I fear that many do not, and from what I hear from my colleagues, they are not only a small minority.

Finally, do you not fear that good communicating is the first service to suffer when people are busy? Surely by causing junior hospital doctors to work the hours they do it is unreasonable to expect them to communicate well.

Prof Baum Most of the consultants with whom I work are well aware of these problems, and actively teach communication skills. There are official communication sessions in both the surgical and medical units in which our psychologists are involved.

I agree absolutely that the first things that are sacrificed to the pressures of time are communication skills. When in a hurry it is easy to frame questions in such a way to get short answers, and yet often one needs long answers.

Dr Hull It may only be a minority of consultants, or GPs, or nurses, but it can have dramatic consequences for the student concerned.

Dr Higgs Telling people difficult things is difficult for everybody, whether it concerns cancer or body odour. The process of becoming a doctor is a painful development. Unpleasant facts have to be faced and learnt. People protect themselves from that pain by becoming worse communicators. We noted earlier that GPs could detect distress in between 20 and 80% of patients. One would get no such scatter amongst the general public. The figures would be narrower and higher. We have not addressed ourselves to the apparent dilemma that intrinsic to medical training is a necessary worsening of our communication skills, because if we picked up all the distress that we were facing, many would never finish their training.

It is bizarre to realise that doctors get so much less supervision and support than the other professions which need to communicate, often about much less unpleasant things than we hear daily. Perhaps as a profession we cannot bear to face all that is presented to us by people who begin to 'unpeel', and the only solution involves shutting down on communication? We must learn professional methods of being able to hear distress without internalising it.

Audience   As a consultant I agree entirely with the medical student, the majority of consultants are in great difficulty when it comes to considering patients and their problems. On the other hand, I do not see why they should be more able, considering their training, and the fact that they are so busy. This is no excuse however for not allowing other professionals, who are experienced and have the time, from being involved.

I am not sure that teaching these skills is as easy as has been suggested. It is an experience akin to developing maturity and integrity. How can you do that in a short time? The difficulty is that a doctor is taught to meet his patients, examine them, and then generalise about their condition. In order to deal with the patients' emotional problems, with their dilemma, you have to do something entirely different; they must become more and more unique as time goes by. This is often avoided due to our medical training—because it becomes too painful. As a psychotherapist I become a catalyst, and stay with these patients whilst they mobilise their own defences, often when no further surgery or treatment can help. I do agree that we need a training which is more experiential. As a trainee psycho-analyst, I had to hold interviews with patients, with a supervisor present, and then give an account in detail of the interview, followed by a personal analysis. I would describe it as a training where you have to be a patient. It would be a good thing if we could all be patients for a while. In my years at the Marsden I saw many colleagues with cancer, and never once have they not said, 'I did not really know what it was like until this happened to me.' Being a doctor, isolated in a nice office with people who protect you, is a corrupting influence. One ceases to be critical of oneself. We need a version of the analyst training where your interviews with patients are scrutinised and your feelings are assessed critically.

Audience   I do not believe that the importance of the communication between junior hospital doctors and GPs is stressed sufficiently. As a Senior House Officer, it was certainly not to me. Often we put the General Practitioner in a difficult position: Despite a full discharge letter, he has no idea of what has been discussed with the patient, especially when cancer was the issue. A closer liaison between the GP and the hospital doctor is necessary. The consultant physician, surgeon or appropriate colleague should contact the GP at discharge, explain the diagnosis and the proposals for management. The GP should then follow up that contact the following day with an appointment in his surgery where he could reinforce that information. We should be working in a team, not as separate entities.

Dr Hull   That reaches its crux in palliative medicine when often we are

64

asked at the hospice to do a domiciliary visit on a patient, but told by the referring agency, often the GP, but sometimes the consultant, that 'under no circumstances are you to tell the patient where you come from.' It is feared that the man from the hospice is seen as carrying a scythe over his shoulder and a sandglass in his hand: the man of death. It is an appalling state of affairs to have reached that stage of an illness, and yet there still be non-communication between doctors.

Audience It is important also that irrespective of what the referral letter says, of what the consultant might think he has said to the patient, or what the GP thinks the surgeon actually said to the patient, to ask the patient of their understanding of the situation. Invariably they hold a different view still. You should not rely totally on the content of a letter.

Audience Professor Baum said that he preferred to be the person who imparts the information about cancer to the patient. I would like to question whether he in fact is the appropriate person. He will not know the patient as well as the GP and may not be the best person to judge how the patient will react. Surely this role that he feels he should play serves to isolate and minimise the function of the GP in imparting such important, devastating news.

Prof Baum Imparting a serious diagnosis like breast cancer is certainly a fraught business. It is emotionally upsetting to the patient and the surgeon.

The surgeon and the GP must have complementary roles. The GP may know more about the family background and the woman herself, but not necessarily. Often these are the first medical consultations such women have had in their lives. There are two aspects to communication: One is delivering facts and the other is providing the emotional support to cope with them. The surgeon is the best person to deliver the facts because he can respond to all the questions. It is quite inadequate to deliver the diagnosis of cancer and then not to be able to handle the supplementary questions, 'What is the prognosis?', 'What is the local treatment?', 'What is the adjuvant treatment?' and so on. The surgeon has therefore the primary role of explaining the diagnosis and being able to give factual, honest answers to all the questions that follow.

Some surgeons, myself included, also like to adopt the second, pastoral role, which exists for the surgeon as much as for the GP when one is dealing with a condition like breast cancer, where you will care for that patient for the rest of your career, or the rest of her life. You may not know her very well to begin with, but you rapidly come to know her as time progresses. For that reason, the very chronicity of the disease, it is very important that the consultant surgeon adopts a pastoral role. In addition, at Kings, we supplement this with a counselling service, because counselling demands a lot of time for listening and one thing that consultant surgeons lack is as much time as they would like.

Audience   I wish to comment on the question of whether the patient (or parent) has to be familiar with the doctor giving the diagnosis to be best supported. Recently a study of 45 families whose children had life-threatening illnesses was undertaken to quantify the effect of this news. The parents gave us detailed information on the way in which the diagnosis was imparted, when, where, by whom, and the effect that they felt that this had on them afterwards. It was not the familiarity with the doctor that was the important thing for them. Sometimes the diagnosis was given by a doctor whom they had scarcely seen before. It was the *manner* in which it was given, the sympathy, the time taken, the fact that the parents were together, all the issues raised earlier. Some of these families actually remembered vivid details of the way the doctor looked at them, the exact words he spoke, 10 or 12 years after the discussion. They felt also that the way they had been told influenced the way they managed their child's illness, and death, for the subsequent years.

Audience   As a member of the Association for Women with Breast Cancer I am struck by the number of women who have not managed to find the person who can listen to them, 12,000 last year. Not everyone has the opportunity of going to a hospital where there is a surgeon with this view, nor a counselling service. Many women in Britain with this condition feel isolated and find the work of support groups essential.

Dr McAvoy   There is a false expectation in many medical schools that communication skills teaching is something that should be done by GPs or psychiatrists; it is a special area that they have expertise in. That is nonsense. It is important that communication skills are seen as an integral part of training in clinical medicine. Students should be seeing good communication skills and role models demonstrated by paediatricians, surgeons, obstetricians, as well as by GPs. We must get away from the idea of peripheralising communication skills teaching, seeing them as something special, and move them into mainstream medical education, and accept that one cannot be a competent clinician, however technically capable, unless one is able to communicate effectively with patients and colleagues.

Audience   I wish to echo the point made of the need to recognise the stress this brings to doctors. I run a support group for paediatricians in a special care baby unit once a month. The doctors believe it is helpful to discuss problems that have affected them and that have proved difficult. It is a delicate issue and one that would benefit from sensible study. It is very important to realise the fears of the carers, e.g. of cancer, like the patients, in order to develop doctors most able to tackle these painful questions.

LIST OF DELEGATES
BREAKING BAD NEWS SYMPOSIUM
20th January 1989

Acquarone S
London

Ajina I
Essex

Aldon P A
Kings Lynn

Aldous J C
Middlesex

Almeida N M
London

Anderson S
London

Backhouse M F
London

Bacon S
London

Ballard J
Middlesex

Barnes P M
Bedford

Barnes S
London

Bentley R M
Birmingham

Berlin A P
London

Bilney C A
Surrey

Blanckenhagen J M P
London

Bor R
London

Breckell M
London

Brett M J E
Middlesex

Bristow R F
London

Broadhurst E R
Norwich

Brown P M
Brighton

Burgess M
London

Burn J L
Bolton

Bywater J E
Berkshire

Cameron I
New Milton

Cameron Z A
New Milton

Campbell P
London

Challacombe C B
London

Chapman P J V
Buckinghamshire

Charmantas M G
London

Cole M
London

Cooney S
London

Cooper M
Dyfed

Corrigan J
Chislehurst

Courtnay Mayers B P
London

Crossley H
London

Cuttell P J C
London

Daish P
Northampton

Davidson E A F
London

Davidson Parker J J
London

Davies D S T
London

Davis-Reynolds L M R
Barnsley

Dawood R B
London

Dean T S
London

De'ath E
London

Duignan M
London

Evans A J
London

Faulkner A
London

Firth H L
London

Fonseca E
London

Francis J
Cardiff

Franklin M
London

Gardner C J F
Crawley

Gillingham N S
London

Goldie L
London

Goose G
London

Gough H
London

Grace E
Birmingham

Greatorex V
Hampshire

Greenbaum A
London

Greenhill L
Buckinghamshire

Griffiths F V
London

Gupta P C
Grimsby

Habel A
Middlesex

Hadley N
London

Hall A
London

Hamblin P M
London

Hanson S D
Exeter

Haran M V
Stafford

Harris L S
Kent

Harris N D
London

Heller J
Surrey

Hicklin K
Wokingham

Khoo C
Welwyn Garden City

Hovey T M
Newbury

Humphrey M E D
London

Humphreys P
Dyfed

Jayaratnam R
London

Jenner C S
Middlesex

Kapur D K
Antrim

Kavalier F C
London

Kay J
London

Kay M C
London

Keys M
Buckinghamshire

Kouloumas G
London

Lang A C
Bromley

Langdon M L
London

Lazarus P A
Leicester

Lefford F
London

Leigh M
Bedford

Lettington L
London

Lettingham W
London

Levene E A
London

69

Limerick S London	Newman C G H London	Reiser S London
Littlewood C M London	Newman D A Maidstone	Robers D A London
Luthra P London	Nyhan E Aberystwyth	Roberts C D London
Marson W S London	O'Brien P Kings Lynn	Robertson P R Brentford
Marteau T M London	Paget S E Chislehurst	Robinson A London
Massey H J O Cheltenham	Palmer D E Brighton	Ronay S Reading
McEwan J London	Palmer S J London	Russell M London
McFarland J R L Antrim	Patil M D Stafford	Rust D Hampshire
McGuigan J B London	Pawley A F Bristol	Ryan D P Loughborough
Meerstadt P W D London	Perakyla A London	Ryley J P Nottingham
Miller R R London	Pizura V A Oxfordshire	Sardana R K London
Mollon P A Stevenage	Pulham N Maidstone	Scammell A M Chatham
Morris P Cambridge	Purwar V Kent	Scott H Bury St Edmunds
Moss C E London	Quarrie J Maidstone	Scott S E Sidcup
Muir M S Cambridgeshire	Rajasundaram S Kent	Sethi K K Hertfordshire
Neve J London	Redmond A O B Belfast	Seward S J London
Nevrkla E J London	Redmond R A A Belfast	Shackleton S C London

Shah K P
London

Shahidulla R
Lincoln

Shahidulla M
Lincoln

Shapiro J
Leicester

Sharma M
London

Sharma R C
London

Shaw F M
London

Shiels A M
Birmingham

Simpson R A
Manchester

Silverman D
Middlesex

Smith S M
London

Snashall S E
Guildford

Sriskandan K
London

St Claire L
Bristol

Stanley-Smith S P
Kent

Stewart K L
London

Stewart T I
Reading

Tavabie A
Orpington

Taylor R G
Kent

Twaij M H
Colchester

Tyrrell J C
Northampton

Veitch Y
Loughborough

Walden F
Leeds

Walker S
Romford

Walton D J
Manchester

Wanigaratne S D
London

Webster J A
Sleaford

Wells F O
London

Weston-Baker E J
London

Wheatley Price M
Bristol

White S
London

Woolley H
Oxford

Yaqub A J
London

Yearsley R H
Kent

Yeo E
Middlesex

Zutshi D W
London

MEDICAL RELATIONS PUBLICATIONS

Current Approaches Series

Vertigo   (reprint October 1985)
Small Bowel Disease
Endometrial Carcinoma
Risk/Benefits of Antidepressants
Obesity
The Biological Clock
Affective Disorders in the Elderly
Childbirth as a Life Event
Sleep Disorders
Advances in Pancreatitis
Sudden Cardiac Death
Neuropsychiatric Aspects of AIDS
Stress, Immunity and Disease

Occasional Papers/Supplements

Acquired Subglottic Stenosis in Infants (Supplement No 17
Journal of Laryngology and Otology—November 1988)

The above publications can be obtained by writing to:

DUPHAR MEDICAL RELATIONS
Duphar Laboratories Limited
West End
Southampton
SO3 3JD